A Bush Theatre and Clean Break Co-Production

FAVOUR

by Ambreen Razia

Opened on 24 June 2022
Bush Theatre, London

FAVOUR

by Ambreen Razia

Cast

Noor	Renu Brindle
Fozia	Rina Fatania
Aleena	Avita Jay
Leila	Ashna Rabheru

Creative Team

Co-Director	Róisín McBrinn
Co-Director	Sophie Dillon Moniram
Set & Costume Designer	Liz Whitbread
Lighting Designer	Sally Ferguson
Sound Designer & Composer	Sonum Batra
Movement Director	Sarita Piotrowski
Design Mentor	Kat Heath
Costume Supervisor	Sabia Smith
Vocal Coach	Gurkiran Kaur
Dramaturg	Deirdre O'Halloran
Casting Director	Vicky Richardson CDG
Production Manager	Tabitha Pigott
CSM	Gemma Scott
ASM	Hester Blindell
Production Electrician	Ola Pryztula
Education Workshop Facilitator	Maryam Shaharuddin

The production would like to thank Funke Adeleke for her help with propping, and Richard Martin at Ridiculous Solutions for the sofa magic.

Cast

Renu Brindle | Noor
Renu Brindle returned to her first love, acting, a few years ago after working as a dentist. She graduated from LAMDA in 2006. Since her return, she has appeared in several screen roles including *Call The Midwife*, Joss Whedon's *The Nevers* for HBO and Working Title Films' *Polite Society*. *Favour* is a very welcome return to the stage for Renu.

Rina Fatania | Fozia
Rina Fatania trained at the Central School of Speech & Drama and has recently been seen as Julie in the UK tour of Tim Firth's *Sheila's Island*. Theatre credits include Susheela Parekh in *NW Trilogy* (Kiln Theatre); Christie in *The Language of Kindness* (Wayward Productions); Brenda Highthorpe in *The Man in the White Suit* (Wyndham's Theatre); Mrs Peachum in *Dead Dog in a Suitcase* (2019 UK tour); Sameena in *Approaching Empty* (Kiln Theatre, Tamasha & Live Theatre); Panna in *The Village* (Theatre Royal Stratford East); Anna Bronski in *The Tin Drum* (Kneehigh Theatre, UK tour); Charlotte/Monks in *Oliver Twist* (Regent's Park Open Air Theatre); Jean in *Roller Diner* (Soho Theatre) and Nanima in *Anita & Me* (UK tour). Other theatre includes Green Genie Uzz in *Sinbad the Sailor* (Theatre Royal Stratford East); Parisa in *Paradise of the Assassins* (Tara Arts); Bindi in *Love N Stuff* (Theatre Royal Stratford East, 2013 & 2016); Mrs Peachum in *Dead Dog in a Suitcase* (UK & international tour); Mummyji in *Mummyji Presents* (Birmingham Rep – The Door); Genie of the Ring in *Aladdin* (De Montford Hall, Leicester); Firoza in *The Empress* (RSC, The Swan Theatre); Fairy Bowbells in *Dick Whittington* (Hackney Empire); Bindi/Sameena Bibi in *Wah! Wah! Girls* (Sadler's Wells/UK tour); The Queen of the Empire in *Cinderella* (Hackney Empire); Abdul/Mother in *Guantanamo Boy* (Brolly Productions); Bibiji in *Britain's Got Bhangra* (UK tour); *The Vagina Monologues* (Alchemy Festival, Southbank); Bushra in *The House of Bilquis Bibi* (Hampstead Theatre & UK tour); Bibiji in *Britain's Got Bhangra* (Rifco Arts); Ayah in *Wuthering Heights* (Tamasha Theatre Co.); Kiran/Ila, characters devised by Rina in *It Aint All Bollywood* (Rifco Arts/national & Pakistan tour); Mrs. Gupta/Ruby in *A Fine Balance* (Tamasha Theatre Co.); Zainab/Hasina in *The Child of Divide* (Tamasha Theatre Co/New York & LA tour); Agnes in *Meri Christmas*, Kiran in *The Deranged Marriage* (Rifco Arts); Pushpa in *Strictly Dandia* (Tamasha Theatre Co.); Swing in *Bombay Dreams* (Apollo Victoria, West End); and Dunyazaad in *Arabian Nights* (Midland Arts Centre). TV credits include *Too Close* (Snowed In Productions); *Wanderlust* (BBC, Netflix); and *People Just Do Nothing* (BBC). Film credits include *Little English* (Resource Productions); *Shawafa* (short, 2019); *Raabta* (Bollywood Film); *Mummji Presents* (BBC Space/Pravesh Kumar); Shammu in *Mumbai Charlie* (Pukkanasha Films); and Agent in *Catch That Train* (Painting Pictures). Radio credits include Big Babushka in *SLAVS* (Hampstead Theatre); *Relativity* (BBC Radio 4); *Bindi Business* by Tanika Gupta (BBC Radio); *Baby Farming* by Tanika Gupta (BBC Radio 3); Meghna in *We Are Water* (BBC World Service); Meghna in *Oceans Unite Us* (BBC World Service); and Mrs. Patel in *Silver Street* (BBC Asian Network).

Avita Jay | Aleena
Avita Jay's theatre credits include *The Comedy of Errors* (RSC); *The Winter's Tale* (RSC); *Lovely Bones* (Birmingham Rep); *Billionaire Boy* (NST Theatre/UK tour); *The Secret Garden* (York Theatre Royal); *The Jungle Book* (national tour); *Bottled Up* (Lyric Hammersmith); *Bring on the Bollywood* (national tour); *We're Stuck* (Shoreditch Town Hall & national tour); *Rapunzel* (Park Theatre); *Pioneer* (Sheffield Crucible & Tour); *Warde Street* (Park Theatre); *Unsung* (Wilton's Music Hall); *The Merry Wives of Windsor* (national tour) and *Sunday Morning at the Centre of the World* (Southwark Playhouse). Her television credits include *Doctors* (BBC); *Emmerdale* (ITV); *Silent Witness* (BBC); *Coronation Street* (ITV); *Down Under Crew* (DU Productions UK); and *L8R* (BBC). On film Avita has appeared in *The Rezort* (Matador Pictures); *London, Paris, New York* (Fox Star Studios); and *Twenty8K* (Formosa Films). Other credits include *Milky Peaks* (Workshop at the National Theatre & Theatr Clwyd); and *Octopus* (rehearsed reading at The Arcola).

Avita would love to thank Fran Wilding for sharing her time and invaluable insights.

Ashna Rabheru | Leila
Ashna Rabheru trained at Royal Welsh College of Music and Drama. Her theatre performances include *The Animal Kingdom* (Hampstead Theatre); *Two Billion Beats* (Orange Tree Theatre); *Living Newspaper Project* (Royal Court Theatre); *Santi & Naz* (VAULT Festival); *[BLANK]* (Donmar Warehouse); *Top Girls* (National Theatre); and *Trojan Horse* (LUNG/Leeds Playhouse). Ashna's television work includes *Red Rose* (Netflix/BBC); *All the Small Things* (BBC); *Pickle Jar* (NBC Universal); *Sex Education* (Netflix); *Year of the Rabbit* (Channel 4); *Bounty* (Channel 4); *Indian Summers* (Channel 4); and *Is This Thing On?* (BBC). On radio she has appeared in *The System* (BBC Radio 4); *Electric Decade: The Good Soldier* (BBC Radio 4); *Bottled* (BBC Radio 4); *Deacon: Moonlight on Water* (BBC Radio 4); *Splott* (BBC Radio Wales); *Dangerous Visions; Perimeter* (BBC Radio 4); and *Where This Service Will Continue* (BBC Radio 4).

Creative Team

Ambreen Razia | Writer
Ambreen Razia is an actress and writer from South London. Her critically acclaimed play *The Diary of a Hounslow Girl* toured nationally around the UK and was adapted as a BBC Three pilot. Her play *POT* which focuses on girls in gangs and children in the UK care system was published by Oberon books and completed a national tour around the UK in 2018. She co-wrote her short film *Relapse* which centred around reoffending after prison. Her screenplay *Romani Girl* was commissioned and produced by Theatre Royal Stratford East in 2020. Ambreen co-edited the BBC Radio 4 chat show *Gossip and Goddesses* with Meera Syal as well as being a part of several writers' rooms. Ambreen was part of BBC Writersroom and on the BBC Talent Hotlist as well as being a member of the Royal Court Writers Group. Recent acting credits include *Hounslow Diaries* (BBC); *Scrapper* (BFI/Film 4); *Black Mirror* (Netflix); *This Way Up* (Channel 4); *Starstruck* (BBC); and *The Curse* (Channel 4). Awards include 'Best Newcomer' (Asian Media Awards), Eastern Eye's 'Emerging Artist' award and 'Best Newcomer' at the Edinburgh Television Awards.

Róisín McBrinn | Co-Director
Róisín is Joint Artistic Director of Clean Break. She has worked as a theatre director in the UK, Ireland and internationally. For Clean Break she has directed *Typical Girls* (Crucible, Sheffield Theatres); *Through This Mist* (Clean Break); *Blis-Ta* (audio drama); *Thick As Theives* (Theatr Clwyd); *Joanne* (Soho Theatre and RSC) and *House/Amongst The Reeds* (Yard Theatre). Amongst others, Róisín has directed for Chichester Festival Theatre (*The Taxidermist's Daughter*); The Abbey Theatre in Dublin (*No Escape/Perve/Heartbreak House*); The Gate Theatre Dublin (*The Snapper*); Sheffield Theatres (*Afterplay*); Leeds Playhouse (*Yerma*); The Tricycle (*The Field*) and as Associate Director for Sherman Theatre (*Before It Rains*, *Sleeping Beauties* and *It's A Family Affair*). Her awards include the Quercus Award (National Theatre) and the Young Vic Jerwood Young Directors' Award. She has been nominated for the Irish Times Best Director Award. She has just been appointed as Artistic Director of The Gate Theatre, Dublin.

Sophie Dillon Moniram | Co-Director
Sophie trained on Mountview Academy's Theatre Directing MA and has been through the National Theatre Studio's Directing Course. She was attached to the Old Vic as an Old Vic 12 director in 2018 where she developed new play *Homo Sacer*. Her directing credits include *POT* by Ambreen Razia (national tour produced by Rua Arts, supported by Ovalhouse and Stratford Circus); *The Diary of a Hounslow Girl* by Ambreen Razia (initially commissioned by Ovalhouse with subsequent national tours produced by Black Theatre Live & House Theatre, and produced as an audio play for Audible); *Midsummer Roman Feast* (RSC); *F**king Outside the Box* (VAULT Festival); *The Five Stages of Waiting*

(Tristan Bates Theatre); *Indian Summer* (White Bear Theatre); *Creditors* (The Cockpit Theatre); *The Star-Spangled Girl*, *Purgatorio* (Karamel Club); *Noah* (short play) by Amir Nizar Zuabi (Young Vic Theatre) and a series of short plays written by prisoners (Synergy Theatre Projects). She has also directed for Guildhall (*Uncle Vanya*, *Three Sisters* and *dirty butterfly*) and LAMDA (*As You Like It*, *A Winter's Tale*, *'Tis Pity She's a Whore*, *Women Beware Women* and *The Falling*, an original audio piece created in partnership with Audible). Her productions as Associate/Resident Director include: *The Greatest Wealth* directed by Adrian Lester (Old Vic); *The Ocean at the End of the Lane* directed by Katy Rudd (National Theatre & Duke of York's Theatre); *The Visit* directed by Jeremy Herrin (National Theatre) and *Yerma* directed by Simon Stone (Young Vic Theatre & NT Live).

Liz Whitbread | Set & Costume Designer
Liz Whitbread has been involved with Clean Break since 2012. In 2019 she graduated from Wimbledon UAL in Theatre Design. Liz notably collaborated on a mobile exhibition inspired by Clean Break's archive, which toured the UK alongside 2019's *Sweatbox*, set inside a prison van, and was then re-imagined as an installation for the retrospective exhibition 'I am a theatre': 40 years of Clean Break Theatre Company, at Swiss Cottage Gallery in summer 2021.

Sally Ferguson | Lighting Designer
Previous theatre credits include *Aladdin* (Lyric Hammersmith); *Mum* (Plymouth Drum, Soho Theatre); *The Offing* (Stephan Joseph Theatre, Newcastle Live); *Anything Is Possible If You Think About It Hard Enough* (Southwark Playhouse); *Two* (New Vic Theatre); *Pippi Longstocking* (Royal & Derngate); *The Last King of Scotland* (Sheffield Crucible); *The Importance of Being Earnest* (Watermill Theatre); *Strange Fruit*, *An Adventure* (Bush Theatre); *Sweet Charity* (Manchester Royal Exchange); *To See The Invisible* (Aldeburgh Festival); *Snow White* (The Wrong Crowd); *End of the Pier*, *Honour*, *Building the Wall* (Park Theatre); *Carmen the Gypsy* (Arcola Theatre); *Again* (Trafalgar Studios); *Richard III* (Perth Theatre); *31 Hours* (Bunker Theatre); *Aladdin*, *Shiver* (Watford Palace Theatre); *Educating Rita* (Queen's Theatre Hornchurch); *While We're Here* (Farnham Maltings); *Jess and Jo Forever* (Orange Tree Theatre/Farnham Maltings); *We Wait in Joyful Hope*, *And Then Come The Nightjars* (Theatre503); *The Sleeping Beauties* (Sherman Cymru).

Sonum Batra | Sound Designer & Composer
Sonum studied music at King's College London, specialising in piano and composition. Recent credits as composer include *The Red Sky at Night* (Milton Theatre, UK tour); *Arabian Nights* (Hoxton Hall); *Relativity* (Finborough Theatre); *Not the End of the World* (Edinburgh Fringe); *Rare Dreams* and *Persona* both for Youth Music Theatre UK; and *A Midsummer Night's Dream* (Warhorse Theatre Works). Recent credits as MD/pianist include *71 Coltman Street*, *Just an Ordinary Lawyer*, *The Railway Children* (Hull Truck); *Aladdin* (Buxton Opera House); *Dick Whittington* (Grange Theatre); *Arabian Nights* (Hoxton

Hall); *Relativity* (Finborough Theatre); *Aladdin* (Embassy Theatre); *Not the End of the World* (Edinburgh Fringe); *Bend it Like Beckham* (workshop, Dominion Theatre); *Bring on the Bollywood* (Belgrade Theatre); *His Indian Boyfriend*, *Kat in Kixx* (Stratford East Theatre); *John and Jen* (Rosemary Branch); *Swallows and Amazons* (Bristol Old Vic); and *They're Playing Our Song* (Catford Broadway).

Sarita Piotrowski | Movement Director
Sarita Piotrowski is a movement director and choreographer working across theatre, opera, TV and film. As Movement Director her theatre and opera credits include *Jitney* (The Old Vic); *The Glass Menagerie* (The Duke of York's Theatre); *Offside* (Futures Theatre); *Theodora* (Royal Opera House); *Jitney* (Headlong & Leeds Playhouse); *The Cunning Little Vixen* (Opera Holland Park); *Tartuffe* (RSC & Birmingham Repertory Company); *A Day in the Death of Joe Egg* (Trafalgar Theatre); *I Would Rather Go Blind* (Omnibus Theatre); *Underwater Love* (Futures Theatre); *Nell Gwynn* (The Ivy Theatre) and *Awa's Journey* (Arcola Theatre). As Associate Movement Director her engagements have included *Best of Enemies* (Young Vic); and *Nine Night* (National Theatre). Choreography credits include *Been So Long* (Netflix); *Reflection Route* (British Museum); *Sher Yadet Nare* (Manoto TV); *Glimpses* (The Place Theatre); *Anything Goes* (Hackney Empire); and *Louder than Words* (feature film).

Kat Heath | Design Mentor
Kat Heath trained in Design for Performance at Wimbledon School of Art and Central Saint Martins. For Clean Break: *Typical Girls* (Sheffield Crucible); *Through This Mist*. For The Bush: *The Burning Tower* (SPID Theatre); *Bush Bazaar* (Theatre Delicatessen) and *Fun Palaces*. Recent designs include *The Third Day: Autumn* and *Audiences of the Future* (Punchdrunk, HBO/Sky); *Fire Songs*, *Sensory Studio*, *The Isle of Brimsker*, *2065*, *A Night Out in Nature* (Frozen Light); *A Curious Quest*, *Punchdrunk Bus*, *Woolwich Hall of Fame* (Punchdrunk Enrichment); *Our Man in Havana* (Watermill Theatre); *Odds On* (Dante or Die); *Il Tabarro* (Copenhagen Opera Festival); *Peaky Blinders* (Rambert); Punk Alley (Moxie Brawl); *Drive Thru* (BLINK Dance theatre); *Dirt*, *WOW Everything is Amazing*, *Fire in the Machine* (SOUNDS LIKE CHAOS); *MSND* (Rift); *The Forest of Forgotten Discos* (Contact Theatre); *The Redux Project* (Richard Dedomenici, BAC/BBC); *The Hollow Hotel* (DifferencEngine); *Macbeth*, *I'm Super Thanks* (Proteus); *Princess Charming* (Spun Glass); *Bridges y Puentes* (Theatre Royal Stratford East); *You've Changed*, *Big Girl's Blouse* (TransCreative); *Così fan tutte* (Bury Court Opera); *The Importance of Being Earnest*, *The Two Worlds of Charlie F* (Theatre Royal Haymarket); *Henry V*, *A Doll's House*, *Shelf Life*, *Chaika Casino*, *A Christmas Carol* (Theatre Delicatessen); *L'Orfeo*, *La bohème*, *Dido and Aeneas* (Silent Opera); and *Girls in Peacetime Want to Dance* (Belle & Sebastian).

Sabia Smith | Costume Supervisor
Sabia studied Costume Construction and Supervision at The Royal Academy of Dramatic Art. Credits include *La Gioconda*, *The Life and Death of Alexander Litvinenko*, *Falstaff*, *Don Carlos* (Grange Park Opera); *Anne of Green Gables* (London Children's Ballet); *Love and Other Acts of Violence* (Donmar Warehouse); *Intimate Apparel*, *Blue Stockings*, *BOY* (LAMDA); *WhoDunnit* [Unrehearsed] (Park Theatre); *Zauberland* (Theatres des Bouffes du Nord/Royal Opera House); *Twelfth Night* (The Watermill Theatre/Wilton's Music Hall); *Emilia* (Mountview); *The Pied Piper*, *The Nutcracker and the Mouse King* (Cornerstone Theatre); *We're Stuck!* (China Plate/Shoreditch Town Hall). Assistant Costume Supervisor credits include *Message in a Bottle* (Sadler's Wells/Universal Music); *Noises Off!* (Playful Productions); *The American Clock* (The Old Vic); and *Young Marx* (The Bridge Theatre).

Gurkiran Kaur | Voice Coach
Gurkiran Kaur is a voice, accent and dialect coach from London. She received her BA in Drama and Theatre Studies from Royal Holloway, University of London before training as an actor at The Bridge Theatre Training Company. She has an MA in Voice Studies from The Royal Central School of Speech and Drama and is part of Freelancers Make Theatre Work's Dawn Chorus collective. Gurkiran works at a number of drama schools and with private and corporate clients. She is part of The Voice and Speech Teaching Associations' EduCore Leadership Team and serves as a Junior Board Member. Coaching credits include *Extinct* (Theatre Royal Stratford East); *Queens of Sheba* (Soho Theatre); *NW Trilogy* (The Kiln); *How to Save the Planet When You're a Young Carer* and *Broke* (Boundless Theatre); *Best of Enemies* (The Young Vic/Headlong); *Red Pitch* (Bush Theatre); *Lotus Beauty* (Hampstead Theatre/Tamasha Theatre); *Henry VIII* (Shakespeare's Globe); *Offside* (Futures Theatre); *Marvin's Binocular's* (The Unicorn); and *Good Karma Hospital* for Tiger Aspect Productions.

Deirdre O'Halloran | Dramaturg
Deirdre O'Halloran is the Literary Manager at the Bush Theatre, working to identify and build relationships with new writers, commission new work and guide plays to the stage. At the Bush she's dramaturged plays including Olivier Award winner *Baby Reindeer* by Richard Gadd, *The High Table* by Temi Wilkey and *An Adventure* by Vinay Patel. Deirdre was previously Literary Associate at Soho Theatre, where she worked as a dramaturg on plays including *Girls* by Theresa Ikoko and *Fury* by Phoebe Eclair-Powell. She led on Soho Theatre's Writers' Lab programme and the biennial Verity Bargate Award. As a freelancer, Deirdre has also been a reader for Out of Joint, Sonia Friedman Productions and Papatango.

Vicky Richardson CDG | **Casting Director**
Credits as Casting Director include *Persuasion* (2022 production: Rose Theatre/Alexandra Palace/Oxford Playhouse); *Rockets and Blue Lights* (National Theatre & Royal Exchange Theatre, Manchester); *Hobson's Choice*, *Mother Courage and Her Children*, *Breaking the Code* (Royal Exchange Theatre, Manchester); *Coriolanus*, *Rutherford and Son*, *Desire Under the Elms* (Crucible Theatre, Sheffield); *Of Kith and Kin* (Crucible Theatre, Sheffield/Bush Theatre); *A Midsummer Night's Dream* (Open Air Theatre, Regent's Park); *LIT* (Nottingham Playhouse/HighTide Festival); *The Box of Delights* (Wilton's Music Hall, 2017 & 2018); *Wonderland* (2018 run); *Holes* (Nottingham Playhouse, alongside Sarah Bird CDG); *I Want My Hat Back* (National Theatre); *Run the Beast Down* (Finborough Theatre); *Henry IV* (Donmar Warehouse/St Ann's Warehouse); *House/Amongst the Reeds* (Clean Break). Credits as Co-Casting Director include *Gypsy*, *Macbeth*, *The Producers*, *Death of a Salesman*, *Queen Margaret*, *The Almighty Sometimes*, *Guys and Dolls*, *Our Town*, *Persuasion* and *Twelfth Night* (Royal Exchange Theatre, Manchester); *Parliament Square* (Royal Exchange Theatre, Manchester/Bush Theatre); *The Resistible Rise of Arturo Ui* and *Versailles* (Donmar Warehouse); *Shakespeare Trilogy* (Donmar Warehouse/St Ann's Warehouse) and *Dedication* (Nuffield Southampton Theatres).

Tabitha Piggott | Production Manager
Tabitha is a production manager for theatre and opera, with a particular passion for new writing. She trained at LAMDA and is now a production manager with eStage. Her credits include *Connections 2022*, *Barrier(s)* (National Theatre); *Red Pitch*, *Overflow* (Bush Theatre); *Old Bridge* (Bush Theatre/Papatango – winner of the Olivier Award for Outstanding Achievement in Affiliate Theatre); *Moreno* (Theatre503); *The 4th Country* (Park Theatre); and *The Dancing Master* (Buxton Opera House).

Gemma Scott | CSM
Gemma Scott has been a freelance stage manager since 2011. This is her first time working with Clean Break. Recent credits include: *The Paradis Files* (Graeae, UK tour); *10 Nights* (Graeae/Tamasha/Bush Theatre); *Last Easter* (Orange Tree Theatre); *All I See Is You* (UK/Australia festival tour); *Zazutinany* (Soho Theatre); *Experience* (Hampstead Theatre).

Hester Blindell | ASM
Hester Blindell has been involved with Clean Break since 2016. In 2020 she graduated from the Stage and Events Management BA course at Rose Bruford. She regularly works with Urdang Dance Academy as freelance Rehearsal Stage Manager and Production Manager on Rose Bruford's Devised Season. She worked as ASM on Mountview's production of *King Lear* in December 2021 and was Stage Manager for *Poisoned Polluted*, at The Old Red Lion Theatre in Angel.

Ola Przytuła | Production Electician
Ola works primarily as a lighting technician focusing on practicals and set electrics. Her recent theatre credits include: production electrician & programmer for *Dead Air* (Riverside Studios); lighting designer for *Barrier(s)* (National Theatre); *This Be The Verse* (The Hen & Chickens Theatre) and *Almost Adult* (The Space); set electrics as part of Lamp&Pencil for *SiX* (Lyric/Vaudeville Theatre); *Moulin Rouge* (Piccadilly Theatre); *Frozen* (Theatre Royal Drury Lane); *Ocean at the End of the Lane* (Duke of York's Theatre); *Fantastically Great Women* (UK tour); *Beauty and the Beast* (UK tour) and *Bedknobs and Broomsticks* (UK tour). She graduated from LAMDA in 2021 after working for five years as a cinematographer and video editor in Warsaw.

Maryam Shaharuddin | Education Workshop Facilitator
Maryam is a facilitator and theatre maker who co-creates theatre with young people and communities in the UK and Malaysia. She has facilitated workshops and performances at a range of organisations including, Almeida, Angel Shed, Kiln, PositivelyUK, Unlock Drama and the UNHCR. She runs a writing group for Muslim Women at Stockroom and is a Visiting Lecturer at The Royal Central School of Speech & Drama. Joy and play are at the heart of her practice, and she is passionate about using theatre for social change.

Bush Theatre 50
EST. 1972

We make theatre for London. Now.

Celebrating its 50th Birthday in 2022, the Bush is a world-famous home for new plays and an internationally renowned champion of playwrights. We discover, nurture and produce the best new writers from the widest range of backgrounds from our home in a distinctive corner of west London.

The Bush has won over 100 awards and developed an enviable reputation for touring its acclaimed productions nationally and internationally.

We are excited by exceptional new voices, stories and perspectives – particularly those with contemporary bite which reflect the vibrancy of British culture now.

Located in the newly renovated old library on Uxbridge Road in the heart of Shepherd's Bush, the theatre houses two performance spaces, a rehearsal room and the lively Library Café & Bar.

Bush Theatre

Artistic Director	Lynette Linton
Executive Director	Lauren Clancy
Associate Artistic Director	Daniel Bailey
Development Assistant	Laura Aiton
Senior Technician	Francis Botu
Development Events Assistant	Sabrina Pui Yee Chin
Digital Marketing Manager	Shannon Clarke
Literary Assistant	Amy Crighton
Venue Manager (Visitor Experience)	Jack Cook
Venue Manager (Bar & Food)	Luke Dart
Head of Development	Ruth Davey
Finance Assistant	Lauren Francis
Theatre Administration Intern (Literary)	Maryam Garad
Young Company Coordinator	Katie Greenall
Head of Finance	Neil Harris
Assistant Venue Manager	Isabele Hernandez
Community Assistant	Valerie Isaiah Sadoh
Assistant Producer	Nikita Karia
Associate Dramatherapist	Wabriya King
Technician (Lighting)	Ariane Nixon
Literary Manager	Deirdre O'Halloran
Producer	Oscar Owen
Event Producer	Robyn Lovell
Head of Marketing	Siobhan Sharp
Press Manager	Martin Shippen
Community Producer	Holly Smith
Technical Manager	Ian Taylor
Marketing and Ticketing Officer	Ed Theakston
Development Officer	Eleanor Tindall
General Manager	Angela Wachner
Theatre Administrator & PA to the Executive	Natasha Wright

Duty Managers
David Bolwell, Rhonwen Cash, Ilaria Ciardelli, Eljai Morais and Robin Wilks.

Venue Supervisors
Judd Launder, Chantal-Carine Neckles, Laura White.

Venue Assistants
Antony Baker, Maryse Baya, Rowan Blake Prescott, William Byam-Shaw, Stephanie Cremona, Molly Elson, Lydia Feerick, Matias Hailu, Giuliano Levato, Moya Matthews, Inigo Maxwell, Jennifer Okolo, Emily Orme, Kathrine Payne, Charlie Phillips, Saroja-Lily Ratnavel, Coral Richards, Amy Teh and Honor Wiggins.

Bush Theatre, 7 Uxbridge Road, London W12 8LJ
Box Office: 020 8743 5050 | Administration: 020 8743 3584
Email: info@bushtheatre.co.uk | bushtheatre.co.uk

Alternative Theatre Company Ltd
The Bush Theatre is a Registered Charity and a company limited by guarantee.
Registered in England no. 1221968 Charity no. 270080

The Bush Theatre would like to thank all its supporters whose valuable contributions have helped us to create a platform for our future and to promote the highest quality new writing, develop the next generation of creative talent, lead innovative community engagement work and champion diversity.

MAJOR DONORS

Gianni & Michael Alen-Buckley
Charles Holloway
Georgia Oetker
Tim & Cathy Score
Susie Simkins
Jack Thorne

LONE STARS

Gianni Alen-Buckley
Michael Alen-Buckley
Jacqui Bull
Jim & Michelle Gibson
Charles Holloway
Georgia Oetker
Susie Simkins

HANDFUL OF STARS

Charlie Bigham
Judy Bollinger
Clyde Cooper
Sue Fletcher
Priscilla John
Simon & Katherine Johnson
Garry Lawrence
Robert Ledger & Sally Moulsdale
Vivienne Lukey
Anthony Marraccino
Aditya Mittal
Clare Rich
Bhagat Sharma
Dame Emma Thompson

RISING STARS

David Brooks
Catharine Browne
Matthew Byam-Shaw
Philip Cameron & Richard Smith
Esperanza Cerdan
Penelope Christie
Lauren Clancy
Tim Clark
Richard & Sarah Clarke
Susan Cuff
Matthew Cushen
Emily Fletcher
Jack Gordon
Hugh & Sarah Grootenhuis
Thea Guest
Melanie Johnson
Davina & Malcolm Judelson
Joanna Kennedy
Fiona l'Anson
Lynette Linton
Michael McCoy
Judy Mellor
Caro Millington
Kate Pakenham
Raj Parkash
Mark & Anne Paterson
Peter Tausig
Joe Tinston & Amelia Knott
Jan Topham
Guy Vincent

CORPORATE SPONSORS

Biznography
Nick Hern Books
Wychwood Media

TRUSTS AND FOUNDATIONS

29th May 1961 Charitable Trust
Backstage Trust
Buffini Chao Foundation
Cockayne Foundation - Grants for the Arts
The D'Oyly Carte Charitable Trust
Hammersmith United Charities
The Harold Hyam Wingate Foundation
John Lyon's Charity
Martin Bowley Charitable Trust
Noël Coward Foundation
Orange Tree Trust
Teale Trust

And all the donors who wish to remain anonymous.

Supported by
ARTS COUNCIL ENGLAND

If you are interested in finding out how to be involved, please visit **bushtheatre.co.uk/support-us** or email **development@bushtheatre.co.uk** or call **020 8743 3584**.

CLEAN BREAK

WHO WE ARE

Clean Break is a women's theatre company established by two women prisoners in 1979 at HMP Askham Grange in Yorkshire. For over forty years we have used theatre to transform the lives of women with criminal justice experience, to challenge preconceptions and inspire new narratives.

WHAT WE DO

Our award-winning theatre productions share the often-hidden stories of women and criminalisation. We are proud to have co-produced our new plays with dozens of UK theatres, including the Royal Court Theatre, Donmar Warehouse, Manchester Royal Exchange, Birmingham Rep, Theatr Clwyd, the Royal Shakespeare Company, Soho Theatre, Sheffield Theatres, and Bush Theatre.

We have engaged with thousands of women on the fringes or with experience of the criminal justice system (our Members) from our women-only building in Kentish Town – a safe space where learning happens, and transformation becomes possible. The programme's success has grown generations of highly skilled and confident alumni, 70% of whom currently progress to further studies, employment, or longer-term volunteering.

'This really is a lifeline helping me to create a new world, a new life for me.' Clean Break Member, 2021

Clean Break has been fortunate to work with many extraordinary writers and creative teams. Our commissioning process offers a unique exchange between artists, our Members and women in prison. Many of the artists we work with cherish their time with Clean Break and have been articulate about how formative the experience has been.

'As a young female playwright, lots of the texts I was picking up were commissioned by Clean Break. And often the plays felt quite quiet; it wasn't about women walking into places and shooting everybody, it wasn't highly glamorised. I really felt drawn to the quiet craft, the kindness.' Alice Birch on writing for Clean Break, 2019

SUPPORT US

We can't do what we do without you. If you'd like to help us use theatre to change lives and minds, please visit our website, www.cleanbreak.org.uk/support

CLEAN BREAK STAFF

Tracey Anderson	Support Manager
Lisa-Marie Ashton	Operations Assistant
Shabina Canon	Operations Assistant
Emily Clarke	Development Officer
Imogen Davies	Individual Giving Manager
Titilola Dawudu	Creative Associate
Nadia Dorr	Communications Manager
Maya Ellis	Producer
Erin Gavaghan	Executive Director
Koonyin Ho	Admin and Support Worker
Rebecca Jones	Interim Administrator
Anna Herrmann	Joint Artistic Director
Emma Kendall	Development Manager
Anja Kulessa	Administrator
Cath Longman-Jones	Head of Finance & Operations
Lorraine Maher	Participation Manager
Mana Maye	Bookkeeper
Selina Mayer	Finance & Data Manager
Róisín McBrinn	Joint Artistic Director
Samantha McNeil	Volunteer Manager
Linda Morgans	Cleaner
Sally Muckley	Head of Development & Communications
Nancy Poole	Press Consultant
Jacqueline Stewart	Head of Participation
Malinda Smith	Operations Assistant
Rachael Smith	Operations Manager
Rachel Valentine Smith	Creative Associate
Dezh Zhelyazkova	Producer

CLEAN BREAK TRUSTEES

CLEAN BREAK PATRONS

Zawe Ashton
Lord Paul Boateng
Dame Judi Dench DBE
Sharon Duncan-Brewster
Sir Richard Eyre CBE
Baroness Helena Kennedy QC
Lucy Kirkwood
Kevin McGrath OBE
Ann Mitchell, Hon.Doc.of Arts UEL
Tanya Moodie
Sonali Naik QC
Yve Newbold LLB
Baroness Usha Prashar CBE
Dr Joan Scanlon
Dame Janet Suzman DBE
Dame Emma Thompson DBE
Dame Harriet Walter DBE
Lia Williams

CLEAN BREAK DEVELOPMENT COMMITTEE

Tracey Abayeta
Honour Bayes
Elise Brown
Sarah Jane Dent
Sophie Fiori
Sharon Heyman
Catherine Hinwood
Alison Jefferis [Chair]
Sarah Jeffs
Gillian Jones
Rebecca Urang
Sara Watson

Clean Break would like to thank all our funders and supporters for their generosity. In particular, Arts Council England, Backstage Trust, Jerwood Arts, Garrick Charitable Trust, Katie Bradford Arts Trust and Richenthal Foundation for their support of new work at Clean Break, and Maria Björnson Memorial Fund & Royal Victoria Hall Foundation for their generous production support of *Favour*.

Clean Break would like to thank those who have partly informed and inspired this story including Clean Break Members, the women and staff at HMP New Hall, Sofia Buncy and the Muslim Women in Prison Project, and Southall Black Sisters.

MARIA BJÖRNSON
MEMORIAL FUND

KEEP IN TOUCH

Be first in the know for all Clean Break's news by signing up to our newsletter via our website, or follow us on our social media channels:

Twitter: @CleanBrk
Facebook: /cleanbreak
Instagram: @CleanBrk

Clean Break, 2 Patshull Road, London NW5 2LB
020 7482 8600

general@cleanbreak.org.uk
www.cleanbreak.org.uk

Registered company number 2690758
Registered charity number 1017560

FAVOUR

Ambreen Razia

My beautiful force,
My walking truth,
My mother,

Who unintentionally led me to myself.

For Mum and Nanoo.

Characters

NOOR, *sixty, Aleena's mother, Leila's grandmother*
ALEENA, *forty, Noor's daughter, Leila's mother*
LEILA, *fifteen, Aleena's daughter, Noor's granddaughter*
FOZIA, *fifty-five, Noor's friend*

Key

Words in **bold** to be spoken in Urdu.

/ indicates that the line after is to be delivered immediately, if seen within a line it indicates the point where the next line overlaps.

Words in *italic* are to be emphasised.

Note

The actor playing Aleena may interpret the relationship with Sian in whichever way they choose.

They may also decide whether she is still alive or no longer.

This text went to press before the end of rehearsals and so may differ slightly from the play as performed.

Winter. 7 a.m. A living room in a small two-bedroom house. All the lights and lamps are on. A television faces away from the audience at the front of the stage. A sofa, with two doilys on the arms, faces the television. Walls are full of family photos. One slightly centre and bigger than the rest consists of a near perfect middle-class Pakistani family: a father, a mother and their two young sons, slightly tilted as it hangs. The room is cluttered with a mesh of Islamic furnishings and Ikea items. A homemade 'welcome home' banner hangs above the sofa, the dining table is covered in Pakistani finger food, the likes of samosas, pakoras, yoghurt, chickpeas, dates. An adjoining kitchen: half of the wallpaper has been removed, half not, cheap appliances and lino flooring. An unkempt armchair sits in the corner of the room. A door frame sits at the back of the stage leading into the hallway and the rest of the house, next to it is a small window with curtains that remain closed.

As the audience enter, NOOR *is anxiously smoking a cigarette with an ashtray on her lap.* LEILA*'s school uniform and bed sheets sit on the arm of the sofa next to her,* NOOR*'s phone rests on top of it.* LEILA *is on the floor, painting on a huge canvas, different coloured paints are scattered around her.*

Lights up.

Scene One

LEILA *continues to paint, she hums Jesy Nelson's 'Boyz', as she gets further into her painting she begins singing the chorus aloud.* NOOR *watches her, after a moment* LEILA *notices* NOOR*'s eyes on her and stops.* NOOR *receives a text on her phone, disappointment floods her face.*

A sudden bang. Something hits the window. NOOR *jumps,* LEILA *gets up, they look at one another before* NOOR *rushes over to the window.*

LEILA. Is it?

NOOR *makes her way back to the sofa.*

NOOR. No.

LEILA *darts to the window.*

Don't open it!

LEILA. Okay I won't.

LEILA *peeps through the curtain.*

It's those dickheads again! /

NOOR. Leila /

LEILA. One of them goes to my school /

NOOR. Come away from the window /

LEILA. That bike's way too big for him, looks like he's mounting a horse…

LEILA *continues to look out.*

Oh my god! /

NOOR (*startled*). What? /

LEILA. He's wearing Kangol…Who wears Kangol?!

LEILA *moves away from the window, she stretches her arms out to the ceiling and winces as she does.*

NOOR. I told you to sit at the table.

LEILA. Proper artists sit on the floor.

NOOR. They sit at desks.

LEILA. I don't have a desk and those chairs hurt my bum.

NOOR. Don't get paint on the carpet.

LEILA. It's been hours, where is she?

NOOR. I don't know.

LEILA. Shall we call her?

NOOR. She doesn't have a phone /

LEILA. What about Auntie Shabana's phone? /

NOOR. I've tried.

LEILA. And?

NOOR *stubs out her cigarette.*

NOOR. Your lunch is by the door.

NOOR *hands* LEILA *her underwear.*

Brush your teeth and get changed.

LEILA *smells her underwear, it smells of smoke, she smells herself.*

LEILA. I need a shower!

NOOR. She'll need the hot water /

LEILA. But I had PE yesterday /

NOOR. You should have had one last / night.

LEILA. I was doing my homework /

NOOR. Did you do your maths?

LEILA. I tried.

NOOR. You tried?

LEILA. It's hard.

NOOR. What about those revision books we bought you?

LEILA. I'd learn Japanese faster.

NOOR. You always finish your art homework.

LEILA. Cos I love art.

NOOR. Science and maths are just as important.

LEILA. Boring…

NOOR. There's some food in the fridge, drop it to your Auntie Fozia on the way.

LEILA (*under her breath*). Can't she come here and get it?…

NOOR. You know she has a bad back.

Beat.

She's your auntie /

LEILA. Not my real auntie /

NOOR. What have I told you about that?

If it wasn't for Fozia we wouldn't have this house.

Don't forget that.

LEILA *smiles.*

LEILA. Don't worry I won't.

Beat.

Nanoo? /

NOOR. Yes?

Beat.

LEILA. Can I have the day off? /

NOOR. No /

LEILA. Please? /

NOOR. **Nay! /**

LEILA. But I have a hundred per cent attendance /

NOOR. And that's how it will stay.

LEILA *huffs.*

I heard your class at the **masjid** has been /

LEILA (*excitedly*). Cancelled!?

NOOR. Delayed, by an hour.

LEILA *sighs.*

One of the sisters has a dentist appointment this afternoon /

LEILA. I'll never get to see her /

NOOR. Don't be a drama queen /

LEILA. It's just one day off /

NOOR. You can pray for her at the **masjid** /

LEILA (*under her breath*). I can pray for her at home.

NOOR *shoots* LEILA *a look.*

God's everywhere!

NOOR. Your routine has to stay the same.

LEILA. I / know

NOOR. That's what the doctor said.

LEILA *huffs.*

Kapray Phenno! Get dressed.

NOOR *hands* LEILA *her school uniform along with fresh bed sheets.*

And that's the last set of bed sheets I'm washing.

Beat.

LEILA. Is she coming?

NOOR. Yes.

Go.

LEILA *exits,* NOOR *glances to see if* LEILA*'s gone, she slips another cigarette out of her packet, lights it and paces up and down.*

LEILA (*offstage*). Maybe her and Auntie Shabana stopped for food?

LEILA *re-enters in her school uniform, she stands in front of the mirror and begins tying her hijab.*

What if something happened to them?

NOOR. What?

LEILA. On the way here /

NOOR. Nothing's happened /

LEILA. How do you know? /

NOOR. I know /

LEILA. How? /

NOOR. I have faith /

LEILA. Faith? /

NOOR. That's all you need /

LEILA. I'd like a phone call /

LEILA *finishes tying her hijab, she looks at* NOOR*, her breathing quickens.*

NOOR. What is it?

LEILA. You know something.

NOOR. What? /

LEILA. And you're not telling me /

NOOR. Leila /

LEILA *begins pacing.*

LEILA. Something's wrong /

NOOR. Don't be silly /

LEILA. I know *you* know something's wrong /

LEILA*'s anxiety grows.*

NOOR. Sit down, **Jaan** /

LEILA. She was supposed to be back last night /

NOOR. Leila /

LEILA. It's too many hours /

NOOR. Listen to me /

LEILA. No /

NOOR. Sit down and take some breaths /

LEILA. I can't /

NOOR. You can /

LEILA. I won't /

NOOR. You will /

LEILA. I won't till you tell me!

Beat.

NOOR. Your Auntie Shabana couldn't pick her up.

Beat.

LEILA. But you said /

NOOR. Her car broke down /

LEILA. How is she meant to get home? /

NOOR. She'll get the bus /

LEILA. The bus! /

LEILA *becomes more frantic.*

What if someone did something to her? /

NOOR. Leila /

LEILA. She doesn't have any money /

NOOR. They give you money /

LEILA. What if she got robbed! /

NOOR. **Bas**, Leila /

LEILA*'s breathing quickens.*

LEILA. Why has it taken all night? /

NOOR. Enough /

LEILA. Auntie Shabana was supposed to go! /

NOOR *approaches her, sits her down and strokes her back.*

NOOR. Take some breaths /

LEILA*'s panic grows.*

In through the nose.

LEILA *shakes her head.*

Don't be stubborn, out through the mouth.

NOOR *begins breathing in through her nose and out through her mouth.*

Let's do five.

LEILA *reluctantly breathes through her nose and out through her mouth,* NOOR *and* LEILA *do this action three times.* LEILA *settles,* NOOR *rubs* LEILA*'s back.*

You didn't take them, did you?

LEILA *turns away from* NOOR.

You have to take them, Leila.

Beat.

She used to play there, right there where you're sitting.

Beat.

My two beautiful girls, her and your Auntie Shabana, I used to knit little jumpers for them.

Beat.

Your Auntie Shabana used to tickle her like this.

NOOR *tickles* LEILA, LEILA *giggles.*

She had the sweetest laugh, it sounded like a thousand little fairies trying to escape through her chest.

NOOR *smiles to herself.*

When your Auntie Shabana was born my **Ami** said that she would be my **Hawa**.

LEILA. What's **Hawa** again?

NOOR. Wind. She said this daughter will be steadfast on some days but absent on others.

LEILA. And Mum?

NOOR. She stared at her for a moment, then sat back in her chair, like something pushed her. 'This daughter will be your **Sooraj**' she said /

LEILA. Your sun?

NOOR. She said she will bring you great joy on some days but will burn you on others.

Beat.

LEILA. What am I?

NOOR. You? /

LEILA. Your moon? /

NOOR. **Nay /**

LEILA. Your stars? /

NOOR. Arrogant girl.

NOOR *holds* LEILA*'s face.*

You're my earth, **Beta**.

LEILA. That's so sick.

NOOR. Who's sick?

LEILA. Sick means good, **Nanoo**.

NOOR *glances down at* LEILA*'s canvas.*

NOOR. Can I see?

LEILA. It's not finished.

NOOR. I don't mind.

LEILA. It's not maths or science.

NOOR. Show me.

After some reluctance LEILA *moves towards her canvas.* NOOR *kneels down towards the canvas, she puts her glasses on.*

LEILA. It's where we're going to live.

It's proper big from the inside, white walls, everything new.

LEILA *places her finger on the canvas.*

That's you.

NOOR *smiles.* LEILA *moves her finger across.*

And that's her.

Beat.

It's manifestation.

NOOR. What's that?

LEILA. It's what you want most in the world, then you draw it or write it down and it comes true.

NOOR *searches the page.*

NOOR. Where are you?

LEILA. Dunno yet.

Beat.

NOOR. Have you brushed your teeth?

LEILA. Yeah!

NOOR. **Apna Moun Kholo** /

LEILA. I have /

NOOR. **Kholo Nah** /

NOOR *holds* LEILA*'s face.* NOOR *looks inside* LEILA*'s mouth.*

Jhoot!

LEILA *giggles, she looks at her canvas.*

LEILA. What do *you* want most in the world?

NOOR. For you to go to school.

NOOR *tickles* LEILA, LEILA *laughs hysterically, after a moment they stop, out of breath.*

LEILA. Tell me.

Beat.

NOOR. I want you, **Jaan**.

NOOR *looks at the wall of photos.*

I want all of you.

In bursts ALEENA, *holding a cheap duffle bag, wearing UGG boots, a colourful eighties retro shell jacket and leggings, soaked to the bone and raging with energy, she flings her bags down and makes a bee line for* LEILA.

ALEENA. There she is! /

LEILA. Mum! /

ALEENA *run towards* LEILA *and gives her a hug, she holds her face,* NOOR *watches.*

ALEENA. Look how bloody beautiful you are! /

LEILA *laughs.*

Let me look at you.

ALEENA *holds* LEILA*'s face and intensely looks at every part of it.*

Yep, he's gone.

LEILA. Who?

ALEENA. Your dad, all his features have gone, give us a spin.

LEILA *slowly turns all the way around.*

Yep! You're totally me, a hundred fuckin' per cent me!

ALEENA *grabs* LEILA*'s face and kisses every part of it,* LEILA *giggles,* ALEENA *clocks* NOOR *but is still immersed in* LEILA.

Salam Alaikum, Ami /

NOOR. **Wa-Alaikum-Salam**, offer your mum a drink, Leila /

NOOR *begins picking up* LEILA*'s canvas and paints and exits into the hallway,* ALEENA *watches* NOOR.

LEILA. I got these fancy cups, Mum /

LEILA *darts towards the table of food.*

ALEENA. Nothing for me, bubs.

NOOR *re-enters.*

NOOR. Some water then /

ALEENA. No tap water for me /

LEILA. Why? /

ALEENA. They put chloride in it, don't they? Closes your third eye /

LEILA. Your what? /

ALEENA *clocks* LEILA*'s hijab.*

ALEENA. Hang about, when did she start wearing that, **Ami**? /

LEILA. About a year ago. /

NOOR. Her and her friend Farah started together /

ALEENA. Who's Farah? /

NOOR. Her best friend /

LEILA. She's head girl in school and in the highest group at **masjid** /

NOOR. Ruxana's daughter /

ALEENA. Ruxana? She was a right lick-ass in school /

NOOR. She was an A-grade student /

ALEENA. Graduated to bored housewife /

NOOR. Farah's a good girl /

ALEENA. Do you really want to wear it, babe? /

LEILA. Loads of models wear them on Instagram /

NOOR. All the girls are wearing them /

ALEENA. All the girls round here you mean?

ALEENA *gets into a downward dog position.*

Good to be home! Freedom! Sweet liberty, mate!

NOOR *moves to the kitchen and begins cleaning the counters.*

Did loads of yoga when I was away.

LEILA. Did you?

ALEENA. Meditation, realigning my chakras, I even saw my spirit animal.

LEILA. What was it?

ALEENA. A cougar.

LEILA. What's that?

ALEENA. Huge cat, beautiful she was.

LEILA. Wow!

ALEENA. And I read that seeing a cougar means you've come into your own.

LEILA. Really?

ALEENA. And that it's time for you to take the lead.

LEILA. What did she look like?

ALEENA. Bit like you, had big brown eyes like you, beautiful thing she was.

NOOR. Leila will pick up your prescription.

ALEENA. I'll be off all that shit / soon.

NOOR. Make sure, Leila.

ALEENA *places both arms in the air, stretches and reaches for the ceiling.*

ALEENA. Green juices from now on, no more caffeine, if it's not from the earth I don't want it in my body /

LEILA. We've got lots of frozen food /

ALEENA. Oi, my girl shouldn't be eating that crap!

NOOR *holds her tongue.*

Sian taught me lots about healthy eating, beautiful Sian.

LEILA. Who's Sian?

ALEENA. Cell mate, soul mate.

LEILA. Can I meet her?

ALEENA *is stunned.*

You okay, Mum?

ALEENA. Yeah.

Beat.

We used to belt out the bangers, Tina, Aretha, Whitney, oh we loved us some Whitney /

LEILA. I love Whitney! /

ALEENA *starts loudly singing Whitney Houston's 'I'm Every Woman'.*

NOOR. Aleena, the neighbours /

ALEENA *keeps singing. She sings and dances towards* LEILA, LEILA *is overjoyed.*

ALEENA (*to* LEILA). Come on, babe!

NOOR. Don't crease her school uniform /

ALEENA *sings the whole chorus.* LEILA *laughs,* NOOR *begins wiping down the kitchen table.*

Belted that out till we got told to shut up /

LEILA. No one to tell you that now /

ALEENA. Got that right, babe!

ALEENA *sticks her tongue at out* NOOR, LEILA *gasps and giggles,* ALEENA *dances towards* LEILA.

What shall we do with your hair, babe?

LEILA. My hair?

ALEENA. What about a pixie cut?

LEILA. Rihanna had that!

ALEENA. We should get you a balayage!

NOOR. She wears the hijab now, Aleena.

ALEENA. Don't mean she can't feel good underneath it. what'd you think of mine?

ALEENA *shows off her hair.*

LEILA. I love it /

ALEENA. Thought I'd grow it /

LEILA. Suits you /

NOOR. Get your mother a towel, Leila.

NOOR *sits at the kitchen table and smokes.* LEILA *grabs a towel from the back of the kitchen door, she offers the towel to* ALEENA.

ALEENA. Cheers, baby.

ALEENA *begins towel drying her hair.*

LEILA. Did you get my drawings, Mum?

Beat.

ALEENA. Yeah, babe.

LEILA. I'll show you what I'm working on /

NOOR. You don't have time /

LEILA *exits into the hallway.*

ALEENA *continues to dry her hair whilst staring hard at* NOOR, NOOR *avoids eye contact, a heavy tension between them.* LEILA *re-enters with her canvas, the tension breaks, she takes it over to* ALEENA.

LEILA. Look.

LEILA *points to the canvas,* ALEENA *can't believe her eyes.*

ALEENA. That me?

LEILA. Yeah and that's the big white house you always spoke about.

ALEENA*'s emotions rise.*

ALEENA. I look like a goddess /

LEILA. I gave you highlights /

ALEENA. Beautiful /

LEILA. There's **Nanoo** /

ALEENA. Mmmm.

Where are you?

LEILA. Erm.

ALEENA. You that butterfly? /

LEILA. Dunno /

ALEENA. Pretty, like you.

LEILA *smiles.*

See that, **Ami**? How talented my girl is, proper gifted you are, babe /

ALEENA *grabs* LEILA *and plants a huge kiss on her face.* LEILA *is overjoyed.*

That's the house we're going to have! /

LEILA. Yeah! /

ALEENA. Beautiful white doors! White shutters, top-of-the-line mod-con shit, you'll see /

NOOR. You're going to be late, Leila /

LEILA. The assignment is manifestation /

ALEENA. Did lots of that inside, powerful stuff, babe /

NOOR (*to* LEILA). Don't forget her prescription, Leila, and your lunch is by the door /

ALEENA *begins examining the room.*

LEILA. What is it? /

NOOR. Cheese /

LEILA. And pickle!? /

NOOR. Tomato.

LEILA *is unimpressed.*

ALEENA. When did everything get so close to the wall? /

NOOR. Don't start, Aleena /

ALEENA *looks underneath the sofa.*

ALEENA. If you wanted to get to that dust you couldn't /

NOOR. I'll get to it later /

ALEENA. I can see it, **Ami**, it's there, and the table against the wall that's just stupid, **Ami**, very stupid /

ALEENA *shoots towards it.*

That'll cause a dent, **Ami**! /

LEILA. I'll move it, Mum /

NOOR. Leave it, Leila /

LEILA *shoots towards the sofa and begins pushing it.*

ALEENA. Council will go mad if they see a dent /

LEILA. It's okay, Mum /

LEILA *finishes repositioning the sofa.*

My teacher said we all have OCD, I can't have my toothbrush facing away from me. That's better, isn't that better, **Nanoo**? /

NOOR *doesn't respond.*

ALEENA. Sian would move everything away from the wall for me.

ALEENA *takes a breath in and out.*

Gaspin' for a ciggy.

LEILA *hands* ALEENA NOOR*'s cigarettes along with a lighter, A shaken* ALEENA *places a cigarette in her mouth and lights it.*

Give us your cheek, bubba /

LEILA. My cheek? /

NOOR. She's very late /

ALEENA. Come closer /

LEILA *moves in closer to* ALEENA, ALEENA *holds the cigarette away from* LEILA *and flutters her eyelashes on to* LEILA*'s cheek,* LEILA *giggles.*

LEILA. What's that? /

ALEENA. The butterfly /

LEILA. The butterfly? /

ALEENA. Like the one in your painting,

Used to put you straight to sleep that did, didn't it, **Ami**?

NOOR *doesn't respond, she sits on the sofa and begins folding the remainder of the laundry from the basket.*

You were in an incubator for three weeks did I ever tell you that?

LEILA. Yes.

ALEENA. You were premature, tiny thing you were, and I just wanted to reach in and snatch you away, I said to the nurse why's my baby the smallest and do you know what she said? /

NOOR. Get going, Leila /

LEILA *begins gathering her things.*

ALEENA. Oh wait! I got you something, babe! /

ALEENA *holds the cigarette in her mouth and unzips her duffle bag.*

LEILA. What is it? /

ALEENA *pulls out an eyeshadow palette.*

Eyeshadow? /

ALEENA. Good quality that is /

NOOR. Where did you get / that?

ALEENA. It's got all the bronzy colours, put the white bit underneath your brow, gives it a lift, you'll make all the girls jealous /

LEILA. They were calling me hairy in PE yesterday /

ALEENA. Do you shave your legs? /

LEILA. **Nanoo** said I'm too young /

NOOR. What's beauty when you have brains /

ALEENA. Beauty's a currency, I don't care what anyone tells you /

LEILA. Farah stuck up for me though /

NOOR *grabs* LEILA*'s rucksack.*

ALEENA. Next time you have to do something, babe /

NOOR. Put this on, Leila /

LEILA. Like what? /

LEILA *approaches* NOOR, NOOR *places* LEILA*'s rucksack over her shoulders.*

ALEENA. Stand up for yourself /

NOOR (*to* LEILA). Get your shoes.

LEILA *grabs her shoes from behind the sofa and begins putting them on.*

LEILA. Sorry Auntie Shabana couldn't pick you up, Mum, **Nanoo** said her car broke down.

ALEENA (*staring at* NOOR). Shame that.

LEILA. Will you be back when I get home?

NOOR. Of course she will, now go.

LEILA *plants a kiss on* ALEENA*'s cheek.*

ALEENA. Education is transformation, baby!

LEILA *grabs her canvas and rushes towards the door, she stops and turns to* ALEENA.

LEILA. What did she say, Mum?

ALEENA. Who?

LEILA. The nurse when I was born.

ALEENA *takes a big drag of her cigarette and exhales.*

ALEENA. She said the smaller the baby the luckier its life.

LEILA *beams a smile.*

LEILA. Love you, Mum.

LEILA *exits.* ALEENA *takes a final last drag of her cigarette and stubs it out.* NOOR *and* ALEENA *are left alone.*

Beat.

ALEENA. She's so big.

Beat.

All grown up.

Beat.

Tall, isn't she?

NOOR. For her age.

ALEENA. Clever.

NOOR. Very talkative, her teachers say.

ALEENA. She's a good girl.

NOOR. Very good.

ALEENA. Not like her old mum.

Pause.

You gonna say something?

NOOR. What would you like me to say?

ALEENA. That I look better.

NOOR. Does it matter how you look? /

ALEENA. I feel better, **Ami /**

NOOR. Good /

ALEENA. Better than better, I feel great –

Beat.

Cut down on my smoking in there.

NOOR. Good.

ALEENA. Helps when you don't have anything to smoke.

Beat.

Did she keep her promise?

Beat.

Did she keep her promise?

NOOR. What does it look like?

ALEENA. Did she get Leila her uniform?

NOOR. Yes /

ALEENA. Laptop? /

NOOR. Yes /

ALEENA. Books? /

NOOR. As you can see, Leila's been looked after.

Beat.

She said she was sorry she couldn't pick you up.

ALEENA. Did she?

NOOR. She had an emergency with the boys.

ALEENA *stares at* NOOR.

ALEENA. You going to ask me how it was?

NOOR *sits at the kitchen table slips out another cigarette and lights it.*

I did a lot of meditation in there, did I tell you that? Hypnosis training, realigning my chakras, I even saw my spirit animal, did I tell you that, Mum? /

NOOR. Yes you did /

ALEENA. 'Give us a fag, Aleena', 'Lend us your toilet roll', 'Quick tug on your vape.' If you look like us they *think* you're backed by your family.

Pause.

It's going to be different now, I know I've said that before, but I mean it this time /

NOOR. Good.

ALEENA. Good? That's it?

NOOR. What do you want me to say?

ALEENA. Say what you feel, **Ami**.

NOOR. What's done is done.

We've moved on.

Have you?

Beat.

ALEENA. Yeah.

NOOR. We have to forget about it,

All of it.

This is a fresh start, Aleena.

ALEENA *stares at* NOOR.

ALEENA. You didn't call me **Jaan**.

NOOR. What?

ALEENA. You always say 'Aleena **Jaan**'.

NOOR. I must have forgot.

ALEENA. Means you don't love me as much.

NOOR. **Bakwas**.

NOOR *gets up and leans against the kitchen counter.*

ALEENA. Home sweet home!

Beat.

Don't worry, **Ami**.

I won't let you down.

ALEENA *winks at* NOOR. NOOR *exits.*

Scene Two

It turns from day to night. ALEENA *takes off her jacket and rolls up her sleeves revealing a tattoo of the letter 'L' on her forearm, surrounded by butterflies. She empties the Pakistani finger food into a black bin bag, ties it and throws it into the hallway, she opens her duffel bag and places pink wafers, chocolate fingers, cheap cinema popcorn and cherryade onto the table, she rushes over to the sofa and plumps up the cushions then shoots back to her duffle bag, she pulls out a small birthday cake and places it in the centre of the table followed by one candle which reads '1' and another which reads '4'.* LEILA *enters,* ALEENA *places the candles in the centre of the cake, whips out a lighter from her back pocket and lights them both.* LEILA *closes her eyes, makes a wish and blows them out.*

Lights up. The same evening.

ALEENA. I can't believe how beautiful you are.

LEILA *scoops the icing off the cake and licks it.*

I'd never tell anyone they were beautiful if I didn't mean it, not even my own flesh and blood.

LEILA. Everyone says I look like you.

ALEENA. That's why you're such a stunner!

ALEENA *tickles* LEILA.

Where does your **Nanoo** keep her ciggies?

LEILA. Handbag.

ALEENA. She won't leave that around me.

LEILA. She keeps some in the drawer.

ALEENA. Get us one will you, bubba.

LEILA *rushes over to the kitchen drawer, pulls out three loose cigarettes and hands them to* ALEENA.

Lovely!

ALEENA *places one behind her ear, one in her pocket and lights one.*

LEILA. What'd you do for your birthdays?

ALEENA. Sian got the girls in the canteen to bake me a cake.

LEILA. Did you get my present?

ALEENA *shoots over to the cherryade on the table.*

ALEENA. Have you tried this?

LEILA. **Nanoo** doesn't let me drink fizzy drinks /

ALEENA *pours* LEILA *a glass of cherryade.*

ALEENA. Well your old mum's back now /

ALEENA *pulls a bright-pink straw out of her pocket.* LEILA *smiles she places the straw in her cup and begins to drink.*

Thought we'd have a little shindig.

LEILA. Shindig?

ALEENA. Party, babe.

LEILA. My friend Danielle calls it a shubz.

ALEENA. A what?

LEILA. A shubz.

ALEENA. Yeah… Well let's call it a party, VIP party, just me and you /

LEILA. I've got homework /

ALEENA. On what?! /

LEILA. Have to write a page talking about *Romeo and Juliet* /

ALEENA. Easy! /

LEILA. Easy? /

ALEENA. It's not a love story, you know? /

LEILA. The teacher said it was /

ALEENA. They don't know anything, I read it.

LEILA. You read *Romeo and Juliet*?

ALEENA. *Othello*, *Macbeth*, *King Lear.*

LEILA. Did you?!

ALEENA. Nothing else to do in there, Sian got me on to reading.

LEILA. It's in for tomorrow.

ALEENA. I'll write you a note.

LEILA. Yes!

ALEENA *enjoys her cigarette.*

ALEENA. Got big plans, you know?

LEILA. Yeah?

ALEENA. Huge, babe, taste some of that popcorn.

LEILA. I'm not supposed to have sugar after nine.

ALEENA. You what?

LEILA. I sleepwalk, **Nanoo** said sugar doesn't help.

ALEENA. It's popcorn, bubs.

LEILA *hesitates then rushes over to the bag of popcorn and rips it open, the popcorn flies everywhere.*

You got strength like your mama!

LEILA. **Nanoo**'s going to kill me.

LEILA *makes herself comfortable on the sofa with her popcorn and her cherryade,* ALEENA *smokes.*

ALEENA. Has your Auntie Shabana been round?

LEILA. She's usually busy with Hakim and Rizwan.

ALEENA. You seen your cousins much?

LEILA *pretends to vomit.*

LEILA They're butters, proper posh boys,

ALEENA. They don't come round?

LEILA (*mouth full of popcorn*). Not for a while now.

ALEENA. And what about your Uncle Tariq?

LEILA. Haven't seen much of him.

ALEENA *takes a long drag of her cigarette.*

This popcorn's yummy.

ALEENA. Used to have movie night in there.

LEILA. What did you watch?

ALEENA. *Sopranos*, *Narcos*, love the mob stuff.

ALEENA *throws herself down on the sofa, swings her legs over the arm rest and lays her head on* LEILA*'s lap.*

I think I was a mob boss in my past life.

LEILA (*mouth full of popcorn*). Yeah you definitely were.

ALEENA. What's your favourite show?

LEILA. I don't watch much TV.

ALEENA. Why not!?

LEILA. Don't have time.

ALEENA. What about the weekends?

LEILA. I do homework, or me and **Nanoo** go shopping or I have Urdu classes.

ALEENA. Bet you watch that *Love Island,* don't you?

LEILA. **Nanoo** doesn't let me.

ALEENA. You what?

LEILA. Says it's just stupid naked people.

ALEENA *sits up.*

ALEENA. There's going to be some changes round here, sugar, and TV allowed whenever you want.

LEILA. Yeah right.

ALEENA. I'm your mum, babe, what I say goes.

LEILA *beams a smile.*

When was the last time you went shopping? /

LEILA. Erm /

ALEENA. Like a proper full-on shopping spree? Shop till you drop, you know? /

LEILA. I've never done that /

ALEENA. Big old shop, nail salon *then*… lunch on me.

ALEENA *looks at* LEILA.

You've got popcorn in your teeth.

LEILA *laughs.*

Right, give us your phone.

LEILA *hands* ALEENA *her phone.*

How'd you get the radio on here?

LEILA. I use Spotify.

ALEENA. Oh yeah wicked!

LEILA. Go on tell me what song you want.

ALEENA. Any song?

LEILA. Any song.

ALEENA *thinks, she's got it.* ALEENA *begins typing away on the phone – Meli'sa Morgan's 'Fool's Paradise' plays through* LEILA*'s phone.* ALEENA *knows this song like the back of her hand.*

ALEENA. I love this song!

LEILA. We should turn it down, Mum.

ALEENA. Feel that, babe?

LEILA *smiles.*

Come on!

ALEENA *dances around the space and sings along to the first verse perfectly,* LEILA *laughs. At the chorus* ALEENA *drags* LEILA *to her feet,* LEILA *is shy,* ALEENA *holds her cigarette in her mouth, spins* LEILA *around and pulls her towards her, they dance loads,* ALEENA *spins* LEILA *round and round.* NOOR *enters.* LEILA *rushes over to the phone and turns the music off, both* ALEENA *and* LEILA *are out of breath.*

LEILA. **Nanoo**, we /

NOOR. What's going on? /

LEILA. Me and Mum were just /

NOOR. Leila, you should get to bed.

Beat.

LEILA. Night, Mum.

ALEENA. Night, babe.

LEILA *exits.*

NOOR. The neighbours will complain.

ALEENA. It's not even eleven /

NOOR. She needs an hour of down time before bed /

ALEENA. Sir yes sir!

NOOR. Aren't you tired? /

ALEENA. My chakras are booming, **Ami** /

NOOR. What is all this chakra nonsense? /

ALEENA. It ain't nonsense /

NOOR. **To Kya?** You're a 'Buddhist' now? A 'Hindu'?

NOOR *laughs.*

ALEENA. I'm one with the earth, the energies. Religion is restraint, **Ami** –

NOOR. You used to say your **Namaz**.

ALEENA. What good did that do me?

NOOR. You're free to believe what you want but you're confusing Leila.

ALEENA. Confusing?

NOOR. Saying her **Namaz** gives her routine, it helps with her…

NOOR *stops herself.*

ALEENA. You can't control what she believes, **Ami**.

NOOR. Islam gives her comfort, don't take that away from her.

NOOR *places her hand on* ALEENA*'s chest.*

Allah yah reh tah he.

ALEENA. God let me down, Mother Nature never does.

NOOR. Mother Nature?

ALEENA. She's the ground we walk on, the air we breathe, the earth –

ALEENA *refers to herself.*

The ever-giving mother.

NOOR *pops her head around the door to see if* LEILA *has gone.*

NOOR. I spoke to Fozia today. There are volunteering jobs at the community centre.

Beat.

Simon said volunteering will go in your favour till you find a paid job.

ALEENA. Why's he calling you? /

NOOR. You gave them your consent /

ALEENA. Well I can do it on my own now /

NOOR. If you miss an appointment you'll breach your probation /

ALEENA. Well I won't /

NOOR. It's just in case.

Beat.

The community centre is easy to get to and you'll be with your own.

ALEENA. My own?

NOOR. Your people.

ALEENA. *My* people?

NOOR. Yes.

ALEENA *scoffs*.

Or would you rather clean some public toilet?

ALEENA. Maybe yeah.

NOOR. In a place you don't know? With people you don't know? Everything is on your doorstep here, and the **masjid** is a bonus.

ALEENA. **Masjid**?

NOOR. Fozia's husband says you can volunteer at the **masjid** on the weekends.

ALEENA. Do what?

NOOR. Community centre in the week, **masjid** on the weekends.

ALEENA. When do I get to see Leila?

NOOR. After you've finished work.

ALEENA. I want to spend time with her.

NOOR. She's busy with school.

ALEENA. I'll be taking her out on the weekends.

NOOR. With what money?

ALEENA. Nope sorry no can do.

NOOR. I want her to see you working.

ALEENA. You want *them* to see me working.

Beat.

As soon as I got off the bus it started, there goes Aleena, the **Sharabi**, alcoholic! One thing these fuckers can't do is whisper /

NOOR. You're being unreasonable /

ALEENA. Oh please, **Ami**.

Beat.

NOOR. Who was whispering?

ALEENA. Ismet /

NOOR. Ismet speaks very highly of you /

ALEENA. She's the worst /

NOOR. She's been good to us, remember that year she helped us pay our council tax, when your father couldn't work /

ALEENA. She walked the other way when she saw me /

NOOR. You're being paranoid /

ALEENA. Everyone's looking at me but you /

NOOR. What? /

ALEENA. You haven't looked at me once since I got back /

NOOR. I'm here /

ALEENA. You weren't there /

NOOR. I'm here now!

Beat.

Getting back on your feet is the greatest gift you can give her.

Beat.

Please, Aleena.

Beat.

I'll call Fozia and let her know you want to volunteer at the **masjid**. They're flexible with hours, if you go on Saturday the sister will show you exactly what to do.

NOOR *opens the kitchen drawer, she takes out a piece of paper and places it in front of* ALEENA.

Here's her number.

ALEENA *doesn't touch it.*

He asked that you call her before you leave the house.

NOOR *goes to exit.*

ALEENA. Celebrated her fourteenth birthday tonight, the one I missed.

NOOR *stops.*

Fourth of July, thirteen minutes past eleven, five pounds, tiny thing she was.

Beat.

(*Proudly.*) Fifteen this year.

Beat.

NOOR. Sixteen.

Beat.

Get some sleep.

Beat.

You have a busy day tomorrow.

NOOR *exits.*

An embarrassed ALEENA *walks over to the cake, pulls out the candles from the cake and throws them in a bin bag followed by the cake and the remining finger food, she exits with the bag.*

Scene Three

NOOR *enters the space, followed by* LEILA *who is in her weekend clothes.* LEILA *and* NOOR *move the finger-food table in front of the sofa,* NOOR *wipes it down.* LEILA *heads to the kitchen, opens a packet of biscuits, places them on a plate and puts them in the centre of the table,* LEILA *opens a kitchen cupboard, gently takes a tea set out and places it on the table,* NOOR *brings over the kettle along with a tea bag, she throws the tea bag into the tea pot and fills up the tea pot with the kettle and places the kettle back on its base.* LEILA *exits,* NOOR *pushes the furniture back against the wall. She walks past the picture of the middle-class Pakistani family and attempts to straighten it twice, both times it falls back on its tilt, she fixes her scarf and places it over her head.* LEILA *ushers* FOZIA *in and exits,* FOZIA *places her handbag down and makes herself comfortable on the sofa,* NOOR *sits next to her and begins pouring tea.*

Lights up. Two weeks later.

FOZIA. Sorry I'm late, I was waiting for them to finish the estimate on the extension /

NOOR. How long will it take? /

FOZIA. Over a month they said /

NOOR. I'm sure it will look lovely /

FOZIA. English builders are bloody lazy /

NOOR. Yes /

FOZIA. We had Polish fit our kitchen, they took no time at all /

NOOR. Fast workers /

FOZIA. Precise /

NOOR. And tidy /

FOZIA *opens the tea pot and looks inside, she observes the tea bag.*

FOZIA. Which tea is this?

NOOR. PG Tips.

FOZIA. We have Twinings at home.

NOOR. Oh.

FOZIA. Funny when you get used to a taste.

FOZIA *reaches into her handbag.*

Here.

FOZIA *takes out her purse.*

Get some nice air fresheners for the rooms, it's starting to smell funny in here.

FOZIA *hands* NOOR *a five-pound note,* NOOR *takes it.*

NOOR. Thank you.

FOZIA. How's Leila? /

NOOR. She's fine /

FOZIA. Is she still taking her / tablets?

NOOR. Not as often, it's getting better /

FOZIA. **Mashallah** /

NOOR. Have some sugar /

NOOR *refers to the sugar on the table.*

FOZIA. I shouldn't, my sugar is very high at the moment /

FOZIA *takes a bite out of her biscuit.* NOOR *watches her chew.*

You should repaint the walls in here.

I know someone who can do it for you /

NOOR. The council were supposed to come /

FOZIA. Don't rely on them, I'll give you my handyman's number, nice boy from back home /

NOOR. Thank you /

FOZIA. I'll text it to Leila.

Beat.

How is she?

NOOR. Fine.

FOZIA. Settling in okay?

NOOR. Yes **Mashallah.**

FOZIA. Has she / been?

NOOR. No.

Beat.

Sometimes I think one of those detox clinics would have been good.

FOZIA. Waste of money.

NOOR. They're professionals.

FOZIA. What will people say? There's no place like home, **Behn**.

Beat.

NOOR. I'm sorry she was late /

FOZIA. **Koi Bhat Nay.** She's adjusting /

NOOR. Ali must have said something /

FOZIA. He understands but it's important the doors are open by four a.m. for **Fajr** prayers.

NOOR. I'll have a word with her /

FOZIA. Aside from that, Ali said she's been doing well at the **masjid** /

NOOR. Good /

FOZIA. If she wants to do any more hours she's more than welcome /

NOOR. The busier she is the better /

FOZIA. It's wonderful that she's at the community centre, they were desperate for people there /

NOOR. She'll be a great help /

FOZIA. People have seen her /

NOOR. Yes /

FOZIA. Saying she's working hard, keeping her head down /

NOOR. Good.

FOZIA *unclasps her bag and pulls out an invitation.*

FOZIA. Anam's daughter is getting married.

NOOR. Saira?

FOZIA. Yes.

FOZIA *places the invitation in front of* NOOR.

He's a barrister /

NOOR. Very nice /

FOZIA. Very handsome, the children will no doubt be beautiful /

NOOR. Was it arranged? /

FOZIA. A love marriage, she met him at work /

NOOR. Muslim? /

FOZIA. Of course /

NOOR. Sunni? /

FOZIA. Yes, **Mashallah**.

NOOR *opens the invitation.* NOOR *reads it.*

You're all invited.

Beat.

NOOR. It says Leila, Noor and Shabana.

FOZIA. Yes.

NOOR. What about Aleena?

Beat.

FOZIA. Anam thought a wedding may be too much for her.

NOOR. It might do her good to start seeing everyone again.

FOZIA. Yes, but it may also be very overwhelming, keeping up appearances.

NOOR. A good opportunity for everyone to see / she's

FOZIA. There will be plenty of time for that.

NOOR. I see.

FOZIA. It's a big day for Anam, Saira is her only daughter.

NOOR. Of course /

FOZIA. And if Aleena felt the need to…

Beat.

I wouldn't want her to feel out of place.

Beat.

NOOR. Of course not, you're right.

FOZIA *places her hand over* NOOR*'s.*

FOZIA. Everyone wants the best for her, but Anam said she doesn't want any tension on the day.

NOOR. Of course. Me and Leila will attend /

FOZIA. Shabana? /

NOOR. I'll call her /

FOZIA. And how are the boys?

NOOR. Wonderful, Rizwan is fantastic at cricket /

FOZIA. Really? /

NOOR. Oh yes, and Hakim is a real ladies' man /

FOZIA. Grandsons are such a joy, Tariq's a good husband to Shabana /

NOOR. Yes /

FOZIA. She's made you proud, Aleena will too in time /

NOOR. **Inshallah** we can all be under one roof again /

FOZIA. These things take time, **Behn**.

NOOR. Aleena says everyone is looking at her /

FOZIA. Tell her not to confuse judgement with concern /

NOOR. **Bilkul.**

FOZIA. Its a lot for our people to understand.

NOOR. Yes.

FOZIA *turns her attention to the armchair.*

FOZIA. It wasn't the same after her father died.

Rasheed was a good man.

NOOR. He was /

FOZIA. Misunderstood /

NOOR. Yes.

FOZIA. Aleena is very much like him.

Beat.

(*Smiling*.) I've seen Aleena grow from a child.

NOOR. We can't thank Ali enough for that solicitor.

FOZIA. It's nothing, he's a good friend of ours.

NOOR. You've been so kind.

FOZIA. **Koi Nay.**

FOZIA *begins gathering her things.*

I had better go.

NOOR *assists her.*

I'll tell Usman to stop selling her cigarettes, Ali said her smoking breaks are constant /

NOOR. Thank you /

FOZIA. The busier she is the better /

NOOR. How is Ali? /

FOZIA. Busy at the **masjid**, it takes up most of his day /

NOOR. I'm sure /

FOZIA. We'll keep a close eye on her /

NOOR. She won't let you down /

FOZIA. Give Aleena my love /

NOOR. I will /

FOZIA. And remember,

Hum sara ekh he.

We're all family, **Jaan**.

FOZIA *exits.* NOOR *is left alone in the space, she picks up the invitation and places it in the kitchen drawer. She begins tidying the cups away.* LEILA *enters, she swipes a biscuit and sits down at the kitchen table.*

LEILA. She always eats the chocolate ones!

NOOR. She's a guest.

LEILA. Greedy guest.

NOOR. Did you do your *Romeo and Juliet* homework?

Beat.

LEILA. Yes.

NOOR. Did you put your bed sheets on?

LEILA. Yep.

NOOR. What about my cigarettes?

LEILA. They didn't give them to me.

NOOR. Why not?

Beat.

Why not, Leila?

Beat.

How much does she owe?

Beat.

How much?

LEILA. Usman said seventy.

NOOR. Go and finish your homework.

LEILA. I can give her my Eid money.

NOOR. Don't you dare!

LEILA *exits.* NOOR *waits a moment then peeks her head around the doorway to see if* LEILA *has gone, she hears* LEILA*'s bedroom door slam, picks up her phone and rings out on her mobile.*

Hello?

Beat.

Salaam Alaikum Shabana.

Beat.

I was just calling to let you know we've been invited to Saira's wedding.

Beat.

Yes she's home, **Mashallah** she's doing very well, keeping busy.

Beat.

It's the happiest I've seen Leila in a long…

Beat.

No she won't be a problem.

Beat.

It's under control, no one knows anything.

Beat.

It would be nice to have everyone together soon, the boys…

Beat.

I understand, a very crucial age, yes.

Beat.

Can I speak to them?

Beat.

I see, next time.

Beat.

Give them my love.

Beat.

Yes I understand, you carry on.

Beat.

Okay, **Hudafis Jaan**.

ALEENA *enters on a high wearing headphone singing Whitney Houston's 'I Have Nothing'.* NOOR *quickly hangs up the phone.*

Did you lock the **masjid?**

ALEENA *sings at* NOOR.

NOOR *begins tidying the cups away,* ALEENA *meets her at the kitchen counter and perches on it, singing at* NOOR.

Usman didn't serve Leila at the shops /

ALEENA *sings on, then laughs, slides her headphones off and dumps her bags down.*

ALEENA. Look what I got Leila! /

NOOR. Did you lock the **masjid**? /

ALEENA *pulls out brand-new stationery from her bag.*

ALEENA. New pencil case, pens, the whole lot /

NOOR. From where? /

ALEENA. And these /

ALEENA *pulls tangled cheap jewellery out of her bag.*

Necklaces, rings, look at this belt.

ALEENA *holds up a fake diamanté belt.*

NOOR. Usman didn't serve Leila at the shops /

ALEENA *busies herself.*

How much do you owe him? /

ALEENA. What you on about? /

NOOR. How much? /

ALEENA. Zilch /

NOOR. Pay him back /

ALEENA. I'll pay him a visit, turning my girl away /

NOOR. And I suppose you bought this stuff? /

ALEENA. She needs things /

NOOR. Stolen things?

ALEENA *returns to unpacking.*

Did you meet with Simon yesterday?

ALEENA *pulls out a jar of mustard from her jacket pocket, she shows it to* NOOR.

ALEENA. It's good for dressing, that.

Beat.

My days got a bit muddled /

NOOR. Muddled? /

ALEENA. And they needed me at the community centre /

NOOR. You have to attend your meetings /

ALEENA. I know /

NOOR. What happened last week? /

ALEENA. What? /

NOOR. Simon said you were being uncooperative /

ALEENA. Still calling you, is he? /

NOOR. I'm your emergency contact /

ALEENA. Well he can call me now /

NOOR. On what? /

ALEENA. My phone /

NOOR. Where did you get a phone? /

ALEENA *busies herself.*

He said you were 'hurling abuse at him'. /

ALEENA. He's a liar /

NOOR. You pointed to a photo of his son and said, 'If God ever made a mistake there it is' /

ALEENA. I don't like him I want a swap /

NOOR. You can't swap probation officers /

ALEENA. Tell him to stop undressing me with his eyes then /

NOOR. He'll put you on remand /

ALEENA. Not if I was at work /

NOOR. You have to show up / that's the rules /

ALEENA. Did you birth a magic child? I can't be in two places at once and why is everything against the wall again?!

ALEENA *hastily shoots past* NOOR *and begins pulling the furniture away from the wall.*

NOOR. You have to be on time with these things.

ALEENA *grabs a dish cloth from the sink and begins wiping down the table.*

ALEENA. Look at these crumbs /

NOOR. Your medication, your appointments /

ALEENA. She can't be doing that /

NOOR. Fozia said you were late opening the **masjid** again today, people need to say their **Fajr** prayers /

ALEENA (*to herself*). Messy /

NOOR. You have to be dependable /

ALEENA. I won't have it, not when she lives with me /

NOOR. Who? /

ALEENA. Mum, please move your scarf out of your face /

NOOR. Take your tablets and I will /

ALEENA. They make me tired /

NOOR. Tablets or the scarf stays /

ALEENA. Call me **Jaan** and I will.

Beat.

Where are they?

NOOR. In the drawer.

ALEENA *opens the kitchen drawer, takes two tablets from her pill box, and swallows them whole, she presents herself to* NOOR. NOOR *moves her scarf out of her face.*

It won't feel so bad if you take them.

ALEENA *settles, kicks off her shoes, and slips out an Evian bottle from her jacket pocket,* NOOR *knows it's not water,* ALEENA *sniffs the arm of the sofa.*

ALEENA. I know that cheap perfume anywhere.

NOOR. You just missed her.

ALEENA. Nosy cow.

NOOR. When I had early starts at the factory who do you think took you to school?

ALEENA. She's been parading our business around.

NOOR. She speaks very highly of you.

ALEENA. Don't they all.

A BANG is heard.

Pricks!

ALEENA *shoots towards the door.*

NOOR. Leave it, Aleena!

ALEENA *exits.*

ALEENA (*off*). COME BACK HERE AND I'LL SNAP YOU IN HALF YOU HEAR ME?!

ALEENA *re-enters the space.*

NOOR. Shouting like that isn't going to help /

ALEENA. We'll let people bash the door in, shall we? /

NOOR. They're children /

ALEENA. They're someone's children though, aren't they? /

NOOR. You can't behave that way in front of Leila /

ALEENA *scoffs.*

Leila needs a mother /

ALEENA. And what chance do I have at that? With you, suffocating us all the time /

NOOR. I have worked very hard on her to make sure she doesn't /

ALEENA. Turn out like me? /

NOOR. Her routine is very important /

ALEENA. She's fifteen, **Ami**! /

NOOR. She has anxiety.

Beat.

ALEENA. What?

Beat.

NOOR. She started screaming in the night, wetting the bed. She was diagnosed last year. Panic disorders, PTSD, anxiety.

Beat.

ALEENA. Why are you looking at me like that?

NOOR. Like what?

ALEENA. Like it's my fault?

NOOR. I didn't say that.

Beat.

The doctor said routine and structure helps.

Beat.

ALEENA. That's what I'm going to give her.

Beat.

I got this plan you see.

ALEENA *walks over to her bag and pulls out some papers, she places them in front of* NOOR.

Beat.

Read it.

Beat.

Worked with the housing team while I was in there.

NOOR *reads the letter.*

Beat.

Tried to push for London, not ideal for two people but we'll make it work.

NOOR. What is this?

ALEENA. They started reeling off Hastings, Suffolk. Kent's only thirty minutes on the train and I didn't want her to be too far.

NOOR. Too far?

ALEENA. From you.

NOOR. Is this a joke?

ALEENA. This is me stepping up, like you said /

NOOR. Stepping up? /

ALEENA. Yes /

NOOR. It's a bedsit /

ALEENA. It's all they had /

NOOR. You're serious? /

ALEENA. Never been more serious /

NOOR. Have you not listened to a word I've said? About how fragile she is? /

ALEENA. I've earned her /

NOOR. She's not a prize, Aleena /

ALEENA. It's my turn –

NOOR. Your *turn*? –

ALEENA. My chance /

NOOR. I'm sure we can come to some arrangement /

ALEENA. Like the arrangement you made before?

NOOR. An arrangement where you can spend more time with her here /

ALEENA. I'll get a job, work while Leila's at school /

NOOR. You can do that here /

ALEENA. Nah, I've done my time and they're making me do more /

NOOR. She's my responsibility /

ALEENA (*raging*). She came out of my body! I watched her in that incubator for three weeks after she was born, do you know what that's like not knowing whether your child is going to make it?

NOOR. Yes, I do.

Beat.

ALEENA. Provided for, you said /

NOOR. Yes /

ALEENA. I saw holes in her shoes, no wonder she's being bullied /

NOOR. You think that's why she's being bullied? /

ALEENA. Why else? /

NOOR. You don't think everyone knows where you've been?

Wake up, Aleena.

Beat.

ALEENA. Shabana was supposed to provide, that was the deal, clothes, school trips, anything she needed.

NOOR. They're just about making ends meet.

ALEENA. Is that why Hakim and Rizwan are in private school? /

NOOR. Don't resent the boys / they've done nothing wrong

ALEENA. Leila would have liked private school /

NOOR. Shabana works hard /

ALEENA *laughs.*

It takes work to keep a family together, a marriage / going

ALEENA. She's your favourite /

NOOR. She made better choices, that's all /

ALEENA. She's a door mat! /

NOOR. Just forget this, Aleena /

ALEENA. Not till I get what I deserve /

NOOR. What is it that you think you deserve? /

ALEENA. A proper start with Leila /

NOOR. No one's saying you can't have that /

ALEENA. A life of our own, away from here. I can give her whatever she needs /

NOOR. She doesn't need cheap eyeshadow, she needs a home, a place where she feels safe /

ALEENA. She's safe with me /

NOOR. What happens when your bills come through? /

ALEENA. I'll pay them /

NOOR. What happens when you run out of money? /

ALEENA. Find a job /

NOOR. Not with your / convictions

ALEENA. I'll make it work /

NOOR. And who's going to manage your appointments? /

ALEENA. I will /

NOOR. How are you going to remember those / on five different medications? /

ALEENA. Leave it, **Ami** /

NOOR. Or when you need a drink? /

NOOR *glances at the Evian bottle,* ALEENA *places it back in her pocket.*

And you have to choose between that and food for Leila /

ALEENA. Ridiculous /

NOOR. It's not ridiculous if it's happened before.

Shame floods ALEENA.

What happens when it gets too much? It will be Leila who pays the price, this isn't what she deserves /

ALEENA. This is exactly what she deserves /

NOOR. Then your hopes for her are small /

ALEENA. Her actual mother taking care of her, that's not small /

NOOR. Uprooting her won't help her anxiety /

ALEENA. She didn't have it before /

NOOR. It started when you left /

ALEENA. 'Left?' Is that what you told her I did? /

NOOR. Face it, you don't know the first thing about being a mother /

ALEENA. You left your own child to rot /

NOOR. You should count yourself lucky /

ALEENA. Sorry? /

NOOR. It was reduced, you were looking at / four years

ALEENA. Don't you dare!

Beat.

Two long years, **Ami**, and we both know it wasn't all mine to do.

Beat.

NOOR. **Sabar**, Aleena, please, give it time.

ALEENA. I've done my time.

ALEENA *puts her coat on and grabs her paperwork, she goes to exit.*

You owe me, **Ami**.

You owe me big.

ALEENA *exits,* NOOR *is left alone in the space, full of dread.*

Scene Four

The lights dim. NOOR *glances over at Shabana's family picture on the wall, she walks over to it and attempts to straighten it again, it falls back on its tilt.* LEILA *enters the space with* FOZIA, *she takes* FOZIA*'s coat and wet umbrella and seats her down,* LEILA *hangs up* FOZIA*'s coat, sits on the sofa and takes her phone out.* NOOR *takes a seat at the table with* FOZIA.

Lights up. One week later.

FOZIA. I won't stay long, Ali is running a few errands, he'll pick me up on the way back.

LEILA *goes to exit.*

How was school, **Beti?**

LEILA *stops dead in her tracks.*

Ismet saw you walking there the other day, you should really get the bus like the other girls.

LEILA. I don't have the money.

NOOR. She's *saving* her money.

FOZIA. Pop over to mine and I'll give you some fare.

NOOR. You don't have to.

FOZIA. It's not safe for a young girl to be walking home alone.

NOOR. Say thank you, Leila.

LEILA. Thank you.

FOZIA. You should say **Shukriya** to elders.

NOOR. Say **Shukriya**, Leila.

LEILA. I've said it.

NOOR. Say it again.

LEILA. **Shukriya.**

FOZIA. **Shabash!** She speaks Urdu beautifully, you should speak it more often.

Your **Nanoo** tells me you want to cut your hair? /

LEILA. I want a pixie cut /

FOZIA. **Nay nay**, you want it nice and long when looking for a **Rishta** /

NOOR. Pour your auntie a tea, Leila /

FOZIA. No tea for me /

LEILA. Bye then /

LEILA *goes to exit.*

FOZIA. A coffee would be nice.

LEILA *stops.*

NOOR. I'm not sure we have coffee? /

FOZIA. Don't bother then /

LEILA. Alright.

LEILA *rushes towards the door.*

NOOR. Leila!

LEILA *stops.*

Go and get your Auntie Fozia a coffee.

NOOR *picks up her handbag and grabs her purse.*

LEILA. From where? /

NOOR. Usman's /

LEILA. I can't go to Usman's shop /

NOOR. Tesco's then /

FOZIA. Like I said it's no bother /

NOOR. Leila.

NOOR *pulls out a five-pound note and places it in* LEILA*'s hand.*

Get yourself something as well.

LEILA (*under her breath*). Earplugs.

NOOR *rushes* LEILA *out the door.*

FOZIA. I'm sorry to intrude.

NOOR. You're never intruding.

FOZIA. Ali is busy with the mosque, the women's section has a leak in the roof.

NOOR. Aleena was telling me.

FOZIA. Ali's raising money to get it fixed.

NOOR. Very charitable.

FOZIA. We've asked everyone for a contribution.

NOOR. Of course.

FOZIA. I've given on your behalf.

Beat.

FOZIA *stands and paces.*

I hate to be the bearer of bad news. But Anam has uninvited Shabana from the wedding.

NOOR. Shabana? Why?

FOZIA. There have been some rumours.

About Tariq.

Beat.

Ismet brought it to my attention that Asma, on Dudley Road, bought a package from him to go on **Umrah**, when she got to the check-in desk they said her ticket was invalid and the hotels didn't have their bookings.

NOOR. There must be a mistake?

FOZIA. When she tried to call Tariq back he had got rid of the number, and Shabana refused to answer her phone.

Beat.

Poor woman, she lost eight hundred pounds. I didn't want to tell you with Aleena coming home.

Beat.

NOOR. I'm so ashamed.

FOZIA. You can't blame yourself.

NOOR. How am I supposed to show my face to anyone?

FOZIA. I thought about that, and we could say that Tariq did it without Shabana's knowing, at least then no one will question you as a mother.

NOOR. Yes.

FOZIA. And I'm sure it's the truth, Shabana isn't particularly thick skinned. I could tell Anam that she had no choice.

NOOR. Yes.

FOZIA. That she's being a dutiful wife, showing a united front for the boys, that sounds admirable.

NOOR. She'll come around when the time's right.

NOOR *reaches over and holds* FOZIA*'s hand.*

Thank you, **Behn**.

FOZIA. You and Leila are still more than welcome to come to the wedding.

NOOR. I couldn't show my face.

FOZIA. We'll fix this, don't worry, your daughters are our daughters.

NOOR. Thank you.

FOZIA. We're family, **Jaan**, it's what we do.

NOOR. I'm ashamed of both of them.

FOZIA. **Behn.**

NOOR. Allah's punishing me.

FOZIA *laughs.*

FOZIA. Punishing you for what?

ALEENA *enters, she stops in her tracks and looks at* FOZIA.

Aleena! What a surprise to see you!

ALEENA. Is it? /

FOZIA. Ey don't be **Chalaak**, come and give your auntie a hug /

ALEENA. I'd love to, but I can't /

FOZIA. Why not? /

NOOR. She has OCD /

ALEENA. Obsessive compulsive disorder, Auntie /

ALEENA *shoots towards the kitchen.*

Repetitive behaviours that you can't control /

FOZIA. Oh? /

ALEENA. So if I wanted to strangle you with your scarf I'd have to repeat it a few times /

NOOR. Aleena!

FOZIA *laughs awkwardly.*

FOZIA. Such a sense of humour, remember those knock knock jokes you used to tell us when you were little? Remember, Noor? She would stand in the front room and make everyone laugh. Your **Ami** tells me you've settled back in? /

ALEENA. Oh yes /

FOZIA. Ali says you're doing well at the **masjid**, I bet it's nice to be back at work /

ALEENA. It's not work if it's not paid /

FOZIA. Well the Devil finds work for idle hands, isn't that right, Noor? /

NOOR. Yes that's right /

FOZIA. Ali says the **masjid** has never been cleaner. Says you've got a real knack for cleaning, I hear cleaners make a good wage nowadays /

ALEENA *slides out some cheese and Rich Tea biscuits from under her jacket.* NOOR *notices but doesn't make a scene.*

She should look into it, Noor.

NOOR *nods.*

I bet it feels nice to be at the **masjid**, Aleena. The sound of the prayers, the **Azaan**, it's incredibly good for the soul, everyone's saying you've really turned a new leaf /

ALEENA (*instantly*). I've been meditating /

FOZIA. Meditating? /

ALEENA. Yeah realigning my chakras and all that /

FOZIA. What is all this? /

NOOR. What she means is she feels better /

ALEENA. Alive! /

NOOR. Stable /

FOZIA. You know, Aleena, people have noticed a real shift in you? /

ALEENA. How can people notice me when I'm not here? /

FOZIA. I'm sorry? /

ALEENA. Believe it or not I'm somewhere else /

FOZIA. What do you mean? /

NOOR. It's nothing /

ALEENA. You've got my body, Auntie, but my spirit? She's elsewhere /

FOZIA. Come on now, Aleena /

ALEENA. Meditation helps you detach from people that don't serve you, you should try it, Auntie! /

FOZIA. Yes well I've always preferred to be in touch with reality.

ALEENA *laughs manically.* FOZIA *looks at* NOOR *awkwardly.*

Don't worry, I've told everyone you'll be back to yourself in no time.

ALEENA. Wonderful. Cheers.

FOZIA. I've heard you've been helping with the flower arrangements. I heard Anam went with the blue flowers in the end, to match Saira's dress /

ALEENA (*to herself*). Blue flowers for Leila's room /

FOZIA. Did you say something, Aleena? /

ALEENA (*back in the room*). I said blue flowers for Leila's / room!

NOOR (*abruptly*). Very unique colour for a wedding /

FOZIA. Sorry you weren't invited to Saira's wedding, Aleena /

ALEENA. I'm absolutely gutted!

NOOR *shoots* ALEENA *a look*. ALEENA *notices two packets of six eggs on the kitchen counter.*

FOZIA. I've told her you're feeling much better, but they just need time to see it for themselves, don't you agree, Noor?

NOOR. **Bilkul.**

FOZIA. Leila will be there on your behalf. She's such a testament to you, darling, everyone adores her, and with everything she's been through she still smiles.

Beat.

You know she reminds me of you when you were a little girl, do you remember, Aleena? You used to come to my house? You'd ask for chocolate biscuits? You would sit on the floor and eat them with a glass of milk /

ALEENA. Ryvita /

FOZIA. I'm sorry? /

ALEENA. Ryvita with jam /

FOZIA. No. It was chocolate biscuits /

ALEENA. Me and Shabana would run to the fridge and down a pint of milk when we got home because our mouths were so dry, never chocolate biscuits / never ever

FOZIA. What I'm trying to say, Aleena /

ALEENA. It was Ryvita /

FOZIA. Yes okay, Ryvita!

What I'm trying to say that you were such a happy child, not a vicious streak in you.

FOZIA *makes her way to the armchair.*

You know it's **gunaah** to upset your mother, Aleena. Heaven lies beneath the feet of our mothers, our children wanting to sit by us all depends on how we carry out our duties.

FOZIA *sits in the armchair.* ALEENA *stares hard at the eggs.*

You should ask yourself whether Leila wants to sit by yours, that should motivate you.

ALEENA *opens the packet.*

I know your father's death was a lot to bear, but he would hate to see you like this.

ALEENA *picks up an egg and holds it in her fist.*

Everyone around here feels the same, we're all routing for you, Aleena, Believe me when I tell you, everyone speaks very highly of you.

ALEENA *throws the egg at* FOZIA, FOZIA *stands on guard.*

FOZIA. What are you doing?!

ALEENA *grabs the box of eggs and throws another,* FOZIA *screams.*

NOOR. Aleena!

ALEENA. Cunt!

She throws another egg at FOZIA. FOZIA *screams and dodges* ALEENA.

She's been spreading our business for years /

ALEENA *throws another.*

NOOR. Aleena, **bas**!

FOZIA. I've done no such thing! /

And another.

ALEENA. A dark cloud over our heads /

And another. FOZIA *screams.*

FOZIA. Stop! /

NOOR. **Bas**, Aleena! /

FOZIA. What is she doing?! /

ALEENA. You make my skin crawl /

And another. FOZIA *cowers away.*

My whole body itch /

NOOR. **Maaf kar dain**, please forgive her.

ALEENA *grabs the other box of eggs.* FOZIA *runs.* NOOR *chases* ALEENA, ALEENA *chases* FOZIA, ALEENA *closes in on her, a terrified* FOZIA *places her hands in the air and surrenders.*

FOZIA. Make her stop, Noor!

NOOR *launches towards* ALEENA, ALEENA *stands threateningly towards* NOOR, *a warning,* NOOR *stops in her tracks.* ALEENA *takes the remainder of the eggs and in one go cracks them on top of* FOZIA*'s head, she smothers the yolk through her hair.* FOZIA *screams and wails.* ALEENA *backs away,* NOOR *stands in shock,* FOZIA *cries,* ALEENA *watches her. After a moment* NOOR *rushes over to* FOZIA *and comforts her.*

You have no shame! **Woh ek Besharam Larhki he!** /

NOOR (*to* ALEENA). **Tum Pagal hogh ho?!** /

FOZIA. I've known you since you were a child.

NOOR *helps a heartbroken* FOZIA *to her feet.* FOZIA *faces* ALEENA.

Your mother's tired, tired of having the entire community judge her based on your disgusting behaviour. Your poor daughter can't even walk with her head up any more /

ALEENA. Fuck off!

ALEENA *launches for* FOZIA, NOOR *grabs hold of* ALEENA*'s arms*.

FOZIA. Yes curse and scream, Aleena!

NOOR. Enough!

ALEENA *violently breaks away from* NOOR.

Who do you think got you your solicitor? /

ALEENA. Oh please, **Ami**! /

NOOR. You should be thanking her! /

ALEENA. Useless pig! /

FOZIA. **Leh!** /

ALEENA. He looked at me like I was scum like I deserved it! /

FOZIA. You punish us for trying to clean you up /

ALEENA. Clean me up? /

FOZIA. You say you're sick but when it comes to the crunch of it you're just selfish, and you think the world owes you something good in exchange for your poor choices /

ALEENA. Poor choices? /

FOZIA. You heard me /

ALEENA. What about your husband's poor choices? /

FOZIA. What on earth are you talking about? /

ALEENA. Beard down to the floor, every fast kept but he still skips from house to house /

NOOR. Enough, Aleena, that's enough! /

FOZIA. I don't know what you're talking about? /

ALEENA. Charity work, is it? /

NOOR. Stop it! /

ALEENA. Fixing the leak in the roof, is he? Raising money for a third world country? If that's the excuse you want to give when you're visiting your other wife then it's a solid one I guess /

FOZIA. She's talking nonsense! /

ALEENA. He's never at the **masjid** /

FOZIA. You don't know what you're talking about /

ALEENA. He's never at home either, is he? /

FOZIA. You don't know anything!

ALEENA *moves closer to* FOZIA.

ALEENA. He checks in at about six o' clock every evening, once he's paid her a visit /

FOZIA. I'm not staying here for this /

ALEENA. A package came for him last week, an eighteen-carat necklace /

NOOR. **Chup**, Aleena /

ALEENA. I'm guessing that's not round your neck? /

FOZIA. Please stop!

NOOR *pulls* ALEENA *back by her arm,* ALEENA *shrugs* NOOR *off.*

ALEENA. They're all the same! Expecting to live in a premature paradise while we suffer and work and endure /

FOZIA. Noor? /

ALEENA. And women like you build it for them /

NOOR. Aleena! /

ALEENA. Because they can quote the hadiths? Because they can give us children? /

ALEENA *laughs*.

NOOR. I won't tell you again, Aleena /

ALEENA. If you think I feel humiliated I can't imagine what you feel, Auntie /

NOOR. **Badtameez!**

NOOR *raises her hand to* ALEENA.

FOZIA. Stop it!

NOOR *stops herself,* ALEENA *doesn't move*. FOZIA *is paralysed, they wait for her to speak.*

I'm sorry if I'm not a free thinker, Aleena, we didn't have the luxury of drinking ourselves into another place, exploring 'other realms', existing on 'higher planes', being disobedient! Maybe if you'd understood compliance a little bit you might have had a chance at a good life!

FOZIA *looks desperately at* NOOR. *The room is silent.*

Beat.

A humiliated FOZIA *gathers her things.*

I should be off.

Ali's mother is coming to stay for the weekend.

NOOR *hands* FOZIA *her coat.*

I have to go to the market and stop off at the chemist.

FOZIA *buttons up her coat.*

I'm sorry to have intruded.

FOZIA *goes to exit, she stops and turns to* NOOR.

It was just the Nikah with her. Legally he's married to me.

NOOR. **Hah Behn.**

FOZIA *exits past* LEILA *as she enters the room.*

LEILA. They only had Nescafé.

NOOR *stares at* ALEENA.

Where did Auntie Fozia go? /

ALEENA. Out /

LEILA. Where? /

ALEENA. For fuck's sake, Leila, it doesn't matter!

Beat.

I'm sorry, baby.

NOOR. Go upstairs, Leila.

ALEENA. No, stay.

LEILA *is torn,* NOOR *shoots* LEILA *a look.* LEILA *exits,* ALEENA *and* NOOR *are left alone in the space.*

NOOR. I want you gone.

After a moment NOOR *exits.*

Scene Five

The lights go down on NOOR *and the house. A big pedicure chair wheels out on to the stage. The lights focus in on the chair so the rest of the space can't be seen.* ALEENA *and* LEILA *enter.* ALEENA *stands centre-stage with her duffle bag, she unzips it and pulls out a T-shirt which says 'Mama Bear' across it, she smiles and puts it on. She takes out a cigarette and lights it.* ALEENA *holds the cigarette in her mouth and begins wiping the chair down with her sleeve.* ALEENA *guides* LEILA *to the pedicure chair in a royal fashion, she adjusts it and makes* LEILA *comfortable.*

Two days later. A dire-looking nail salon. LEILA *is sat facing the audience with her hands out and feet up, extremely happy and content.*

ALEENA. You like it?

LEILA. I've never had a manicure.

ALEENA. You haven't lived.

LEILA. All the girls in my school have them.

ALEENA. Won't be as nice as yours, babe.

LEILA. They get fake ones at school.

ALEENA. You don't need those.

LEILA. Don't I?

ALEENA. Nah, you got beautiful long fingers, like your mama.

LEILA. Do you think?

ALEENA. The girls at your school probably have short stubby fingers.

LEILA. Yeah they do actually!

ALEENA. There you go darlin', making up for lost features.

LEILA *smiles.*

How's the chair?

LEILA. It's alright.

ALEENA. Doesn't look great.

ALEENA *inspects the chair.*

Needs a bit of something.

LEILA. Like what?

ALEENA. Bit of style.

LEILA. How'd you give a chair style?

ALEENA. Wanna see, bubs?

LEILA. Yeah go on.

ALEENA *clicks her fingers, the chair lights up,* LEILA *is beside herself.*

Whoa!

ALEENA. See that.

LEILA. How did you?!

ALEENA. Stick with me, bubba.

LEILA. That's sick!

ALEENA. Only the best for you.

LEILA. What colour you getting, Mum?

ALEENA. Don't you worry about me.

LEILA. Why?

ALEENA. This is your day.

LEILA giggles.

You tell me what you want, babe?

LEILA. Anything? /

ALEENA. Anything! /

LEILA. I could do with a drink /

ALEENA. Girl after my own heart, what do you want? /

LEILA. I don't know /

ALEENA. Oh come on, babe!

LEILA. Erm… a mocktail?

ALEENA. Nice choice which one? /

LEILA. Mango? /

ALEENA. Mango it is!

ALEENA clicks her fingers, LEILA feels a jolt under her right arm, she opens the arm rest and pulls out a bright mango mocktail with a straw.

LEILA. Wow!

ALEENA. Taste it.

LEILA takes a long slurp through the straw.

LEILA. That's yum /

ALEENA. Whoever said your mama couldn't get you anything /

LEILA beams a huge smile, admires her nails, and enjoys her mocktail.

When you were little you used to have this dip in the back of your neck /

LEILA. Did I? /

ALEENA. Yeah proper little slope. I used to plant about a hundred kisses on it a day /

LEILA. I remember /

ALEENA. And I used to tickle your ears to put you to sleep /

LEILA. Did you sing me a lullaby? /

ALEENA. Yeah! Well. Whitney.

LEILA. What else are we gonna do?

ALEENA. Anything you want, babe!

LEILA. Anything?

ALEENA. You name it.

LEILA. What about high tea like the Queen has?

ALEENA. Now you're talking.

LEILA. And we can wear tiaras?

ALEENA. Done.

ALEENA *clicks both her fingers.* LEILA *feels another jolt under her left arm, she opens the other arm rest, inside sits a tiara. She gasps at it. An ecstatic* LEILA *places it on her head.*

LEILA. That's well pretty.

ALEENA. So, Queen Leila, what about a car?

LEILA. A car?

ALEENA. A nice little Mercedes A-Class, proper rims, speaker system the lot.

LEILA. I can't drive yet.

ALEENA. I'll teach you how to drive.

LEILA. Can you drive now, Mum?

ALEENA. What'd you mean?

LEILA. You're on a ban.

ALEENA. Alright, babe, don't shout it out…

LEILA *laughs.*

What else? /

LEILA *gasps*.

LEILA. Nando's! /

ALEENA. Nando's? /

LEILA. I love Nando's /

ALEENA. You can do better than that /

LEILA. I don't want you spending loads /

ALEENA. Don't you worry about that, come on, babe, think big /

LEILA. Erm…

ALEENA. Anything or anywhere in the world! /

LEILA. Erm /

ALEENA. Don't be shy.

LEILA. I've always wanted to go to…

ALEENA. The Bahamas? /

LEILA. America /

ALEENA. Lovely! /

LEILA (*in an Italian American accent*). New York /

ALEENA. The Big Apple, baby /

LEILA. I want to go to Broadway! Can we see the Statue of Liberty?! /

ALEENA. Yeah, baby, you'll love it /

LEILA. Will I? /

ALEENA. A woman holding her flame, owning her shit, what's not to love?

ALEENA *gets up and looks at the ceiling*.

LEILA. What is it?

ALEENA *contemplates the space*.

ALEENA. Bit dark in here.

LEILA. Is it?

ALEENA. Needs something.

LEILA. Like what?

ALEENA. A countdown, babe.

LEILA. A what?

ALEENA. A countdown.

From five.

LEILA. Okay.

ALEENA. Five /

LEILA. Four /

ALEENA. Three, two, one. LEILA. Three, two, one.

A bright candyfloss-pink light spills out across the stage, lighting up the whole salon, magical in its presence. Meditative spa music plays.

LEILA. How did you?!

ALEENA. Super woman, me.

LEILA. Oh let's take a selfie!

ALEENA. Oh yeah, go on, I love those!

LEILA *pulls out her phone.*

LEILA. Come here, Mum!

LEILA *points the camera directly at them, they pose,* LEILA *takes a picture,* ALEENA *looks at it.*

ALEENA. That's wicked that is!

LEILA. Now do a silly one!

LEILA *and* ALEENA *both pull a silly face.*

Love it.

LEILA *notices her nails, she huffs.*

ALEENA. What's wrong, baby? /

LEILA. I'm not sure about this purple /

ALEENA. What you on about? It's lovely! /

LEILA. I should have gone with what you said /

ALEENA. Yellow? /

LEILA. Yeah /

ALEENA. Like the sun /

LEILA. Yeah /

ALEENA. No worries, babe /

ALEENA *clicks her fingers*. LEILA*'s nail colour changes to a bright yellow.*

LEILA. Wow! Thanks, Mum /

ALEENA. Don't mention it /

LEILA. You're brilliant today /

ALEENA. I think I've got my mojo back, Leila, it's all looking up.

LEILA. I love you, Mum.

ALEENA. I love you more.

LEILA. How much?

ALEENA. I love you so much, my girl, my heart could burst.

LEILA. I'm glad you're better.

ALEENA. I'm feeling on top of the world!

LEILA. Same!

ALEENA. I'm gonna be the best mum ever, you'll see.

LEILA *giggles.*

No I mean it, babe! I'm gonna do all the proper mum stuff, you know?

LEILA. Mum stuff? /

ALEENA. Yeah, like dropping you to school /

LEILA. I walk to school on my own now, Mum /

ALEENA. Helping you choose your colleges /

LEILA. Yeah? /

ALEENA. Beating down the boy who breaks your heart /

LEILA. That'll never happen /

ALEENA. Oh there will be a boy /

LEILA. Pffff /

ALEENA *sits on the wheelie chair and spins around on it like a big kid.*

ALEENA. A boy who will knock you right off your feet, he'll cut through all the shit and get you right where it hurts, you'll feel swept up one minute and crushed the next.

LEILA. Why don't we ever talk about Dad?

ALEENA. Don't have to.

LEILA. Why?

ALEENA. Because you're my baby!

ALEENA *grabs* LEILA*'s cheek and kisses it multiple times.* LEILA *giggles.*

My baby and no one else's.

LEILA. I'll be careful with the boys I choose.

ALEENA. Don't be, fall in love, get your heart broken, live, my girl.

LEILA. Alright. ALEENA. Alright?

ALEENA. Make a wish! /

LEILA. A wish? /

ALEENA. If you say a word at the same time as someone else you make a wish /

LEILA. Okay /

ALEENA. And say it aloud! /

LEILA. Will it come true? /

ALEENA. Of course it will!

Beat

LEILA. I wish that you stay with me forever /

ALEENA. Snap! I wished that too, babe /

LEILA. Did you? /

ALEENA. That's mad! /

LEILA. Yeah it is!

Beat.

ALEENA. You know what I've realised, babe?

LEILA. What?

ALEENA. God doesn't answer your wishes, people do…

LEILA. **Nanoo** says Allah always listens.

ALEENA. Yeah but not straight away.

ALEENA *kneels next to* LEILA.

You see what just happened there? I answered your wish and you answered mine, instant, babe!

LEILA. What if we can't answer each other's, what if it's too big?

ALEENA. I'm going to answer all your wishes, bubba! Big or small, it'll be me who makes them come true, no one else.

ALEENA *tickles* LEILA, LEILA *giggles*. ALEENA *gets up*.

There's so much to plan /

LEILA. Plan? /

ALEENA. The two of us, mother and daughter taking on the world /

LEILA. I can't wait /

ALEENA. Waking up together /

LEILA. Yeah /

ALEENA. Leave the house without being stared at /

LEILA. That would be nice /

ALEENA. Anything's possible, bubba.

LEILA. Yeah!

ALEENA. Movie weekends.

LEILA. If **Nanoo** lets us watch the TV.

Pause.

The spa music stops.

ALEENA. What if we didn't have to ask anyone's permission?

LEILA. We have to ask **Nanoo**.

ALEENA. What if we could do whatever we want whenever we want?

Beat.

What if on a Friday you didn't want to go to the **masjid**?

LEILA. I have to.

ALEENA. But what if one day you just wanted to binge your favourite TV show.

LEILA. *Orange is the New Black*?

ALEENA. Or listen to your favourite tunes?

LEILA. **Nanoo** says I need routine.

ALEENA. Not always.

LEILA. She says I need it to feel better.

ALEENA. Your **Nanoo** isn't right about everything.

LEILA. It would make **Nanoo** sad if I didn't go to **masjid**… and I like it!

Beat.

ALEENA. What if **Nanoo** wasn't there any more?

Beat.

The pink lighting begins to slowly dim.

What if we could live together, just us.

Beat.

I've got a new place.

LEILA. A new place?

ALEENA. It's small /

LEILA. Oh /

ALEENA. But cosy /

LEILA. Where is it?

ALEENA. In Kent.

LEILA. Kent?

Beat.

The pink lighting dims further.

ALEENA. I know it's not London but /

LEILA. Kent's far /

ALEENA. Not that far /

LEILA. What about my friends? /

ALEENA. You can make new friends, babe /

LEILA. What about **Nanoo**? /

ALEENA. She's looked after you long enough /

LEILA. I don't want her to be on her own /

ALEENA. We'll visit her all the time /

LEILA. Yeah but…

ALEENA *kneels down and looks up at* LEILA.

ALEENA. I know it's scary, babe, but I'm better now, I want us to have a future together, I don't want anyone getting in the way.

LEILA. What if I don't like Kent?

ALEENA. It's so much nicer, babe, we'll be closer to the sea!

LEILA. I like London.

The pink lighting dims further.

ALEENA. I'll set up your own little desk for you /

LEILA. What about school? /

ALEENA. They've got schools there.

Beat.

Don't you want to live with me? /

LEILA. I do, Mum, I do.

ALEENA *gets up.*

ALEENA. This is our chance! /

LEILA. It's a bit scary though /

ALEENA. It's a new start, an adventure /

LEILA. I don't know, Mum /

ALEENA. I won't mess up again /

LEILA. I know / but

ALEENA. I know that's what you're scared of but my time away, Leila, it's really sorted me out!

The pink lighting dims further.

LEILA. I don't want to leave London! /

ALEENA. London ain't all that /

LEILA. I like Ilford /

ALEENA. No one likes Ilford, babe /

LEILA. I don't like change /

ALEENA. Change is good, bubba /

LEILA. It scares me /

ALEENA. You don't have to be scared, not any more /

LEILA. I don't want to leave **Nanoo** /

ALEENA. She'll be alright /

LEILA. Who's going to look after her /

ALEENA. All she's ever wanted is for me to look after you /

The pink lighting dims further, the stage is almost in its natural lighting state. ALEENA *grabs* LEILA*'s hands.*

Please, Leila /

LEILA. My nails, Mum! /

ALEENA. Listen to me /

LEILA. Okay /

ALEENA. Are you listening? /

LEILA. Yes, Mum /

ALEENA *releases* LEILA*'s hands, she holds her shoulders tightly and looks at her.*

ALEENA. I'm going to be honest with you, Leila.

ALEENA *doesn't let go, manic now.*

If I stay at **Nanoo**'s I'll get sick again, they'll make me sick /

LEILA. Who? /

ALEENA. Everyone, they're nasty round here /

LEILA. Not everyone is, Mum! /

ALEENA. They won't let me breathe here /

ALEENA *lets go of* LEILA *and begins pacing.*

LEILA. The sister who teaches me at the **masjid** always asks about you, some people really care /

ALEENA. Most don't, babe /

LEILA. But some do /

ALEENA. I love you, Leila /

LEILA. I know, Mum /

ALEENA *grips* LEILA*'s shoulders and pulls her towards her.*

ALEENA. I love you more than anyone /

And you love me, don't you? /

LEILA. You're hurting me, Mum /

ALEENA. Don't you, babe? /

LEILA. Yes /

ALEENA. So we shouldn't be with anyone else but each other /

LEILA. Yeah but /

ALEENA. I'm so sorry, baby, I'm sorry for everything I've done, everything I've put you through /

ALEENA *collapses on the floor of the nail salon and begins to cry.*

I can't stay here /

LEILA. Mum, please /

ALEENA. I really need you, Leila /

LEILA. I'm here /

ALEENA. I can't be alone /

LEILA. Okay /

ALEENA. I can't be by myself /

LEILA. What'd you mean? /

ALEENA. If you don't come with me, Leila, I don't know what I'll do –

LEILA. Stop it, Mum!

LEILA *gets up.*

Pause.

The stage has returned to its natural lighting state.

LEILA *joins* ALEENA *on the floor and hugs her.*

ALEENA. They want me to disappear.

LEILA. Who?

ALEENA. So I tried, I tried to disappear.

LEILA. Mum, you're scaring me.

ALEENA. I'm not saying this to scare you.

LEILA. But you are

ALEENA. I just love you so much, you're my baby.

Please, Leila, I don't know what I'll do, don't leave me.

ALEENA *begins to sob in* LEILA*'s lap.*

Beat.

LEILA. Okay, Mum, stop crying.

LEILA *strokes* ALEENA*'s head.*

I'll come with you.

Beat.

Please stop crying.

The pedicure-chair lights snap off.

LEILA *lifts* ALEENA *up and hugs her tightly.*

Scene Six

NOOR *enters the space with her headscarf on, she reaches behind the sofa and pulls out her prayer mat, she lays it down, stands on it and begins saying her Namaz.* ALEENA *stands just outside the space, almost condemned from it. She slips out a cigarette, lights it and smokes manically.* LEILA *reaches behind the sofa, she lays out her canvas and paints and begins rubbing her painting out, also manically.* ALEENA *and* LEILA *continue their manic action until the end of* NOOR*'s prayer.* ALEENA *stubs her cigarette out and exits. The lights slowly come up on* LEILA *and* NOOR *back in* NOOR*'s house.* NOOR *finalises her prayer and turns her head to the left and then to the right.*

Two days later. NOOR *sits on her prayer mat and watches* LEILA *aggressively rubbing across her canvas with paint stripper.*

LEILA. Farah couldn't come this morning, they've got family over from Karachi.

NOOR. Will you get to see her before you go?

LEILA *shrugs.*

LEILA. She's been weird with me since Mum came back.

LEILA *continues rubbing.*

She doesn't talk to me at **masjid** any more and she always sits with Mariam and the other girls, she said her mum doesn't want her round here right now, and that she was 'really sad about it'.

LEILA *rubs the canvas harder.*

She's changed since she started contouring anyway.

NOOR. You shouldn't fall out with her.

LEILA. I won't see her anyway.

NOOR *picks up her Jaan Namaz and places it behind the sofa.*

NOOR. You'll ruin it.

LEILA. I don't care!

LEILA*'s canvas rips,* LEILA *throws the cloth across the room in a rage.*

NOOR. You're just tired, **Jaan** /

LEILA. I'm tired of you!

Beat.

NOOR. I'll speak to your teacher at parents' evening.

LEILA. It's called parents' evening not grandma evening! And do you know what? I'd be better at maths if someone sat down and taught it to me like Farah's mum does.

LEILA *picks up her canvas and places it against the wall, she begins tidying her paints away.*

At least in Kent I can go to the cinema, and go to house parties and wear shorts in the summer /

NOOR. And that will make you happy? Going to the cinema in shorts? /

LEILA. I'm outgrowing this place anyway, like Jesy Nelson with Little Mix, at least I'll be able to go to the shops without being stared at.

Beat.

(*Gloating.*) She said she's going to get me a desk with a pull-out chair, so I won't have to do my work on my bed any more and I looked on Google and it looks well nice, lots of parks, it's less noisy there, not like London and she said she'll come to all of my parents' evenings /

NOOR. What about your friends? /

LEILA. I'll find new friends /

NOOR. School? /

LEILA. They've got good schools, anyway London's overrated, everyone's moving out now.

Beat.

There's a beach there, with really pretty water and…

LEILA *stops. She cries.* NOOR *hugs* LEILA.

NOOR. **Bas**, **Jaan**, don't cry.

NOOR *grips* LEILA*'s arms and looks at her.*

This is your home, Leila. This will always be your home.

LEILA *winces and walks away from* NOOR, LEILA *sits on the sofa,* NOOR *stares at her.*

Beat.

Let me see.

LEILA. See what?

Beat.

NOOR. Take it off.

LEILA *touches her shoulder.*

Now.

LEILA. It was an accident!

NOOR. She hurt you?

Beat.

ALEENA *enters on a high with her duffle bag, she throws it down.*

ALEENA. I'm thinking white!

ALEENA *grabs her jacket and puts it on.*

White walls, white ceiling, duck-blue furniture, make it look all French? French is the shit, babe, classy, and I don't want to overcrowd the place, few nice pieces here and there, lamps, lots of lamps! For my SAD, blinds!

ALEENA *grabs her shoes and slips them on.*

No shitty curtains and I'll get you a beautiful mirror where you can do your make-up /

LEILA. Yeah… –

ALEENA. Sen-fuckin-sational, bubba!

This is it, me and you!

ALEENA *rushes over to* LEILA *and gives her a huge kiss on her cheek.*

I was thinking I'd get a job in a travel agent's /

LEILA. Yeah… /

ALEENA. Closest I can get to my old job as an air hostess, we can get discounts on holidays /

NOOR *begins to laugh.*

Law of attraction, say it enough and it'll happen /

NOOR *continues to laugh.*

Travelled the world as an air hostess!

ALEENA *attempts to carry on through* NOOR*'s laughter.*

You had to be a bloody beauty queen when I was in the air.

ALEENA *and* LEILA *watch* NOOR *hysterically laugh.*

What's so funny, **Ami**? /

NOOR. I was just thinking /

ALEENA. What? /

NOOR. What did I ever do to deserve such a clown for a daughter /

ALEENA. What did you call me? /

NOOR *continues to laugh.*

Come on, Leila.

NOOR *stops and gathers herself.*

NOOR. You're hysterical you really are /

ALEENA. Don't laugh at me! /

NOOR. French furniture, Aleena? /

ALEENA. Come on, bubs /

NOOR. You can't even take her on a day out /

ALEENA. This is happening, **Ami**, get used to it /

NOOR. You're too blind to see it for yourself, aren't you? /

ALEENA. See what?

NOOR *rushes over to* LEILA *and grabs her.*

LEILA. What are you doing?!

NOOR *pulls* LEILA*'s top down to reveal the bruises on her shoulder.*

Stop it!

ALEENA *stands paralysed.* LEILA *snatches herself away from* NOOR. *Shame floods* ALEENA. *A humiliated* LEILA *rushes to the sofa.*

ALEENA. Leila? /

LEILA *cowers away.*

NOOR. Face it, Aleena, you're a danger to her /

ALEENA. Where's your case, babe? /

ALEENA *heads to the door,* NOOR *stands in her path.*

NOOR. She stays here /

ALEENA. For what?! To have a half-assed wedding with some nobody's son? /

NOOR. I want her to have an education, I want her to have options /

ALEENA. Bollocks you do /

NOOR. Whatever it takes to protect her / I'll do it

ALEENA. The only person she needs protection from is you /

NOOR. Child services will take one look / at her arm

ALEENA. What did you say? /

NOOR. If you don't leave now you won't see her again /

ALEENA. You won't do this again /

NOOR. Go upstairs, Leila /

ALEENA. You won't keep us apart /

NOOR. Go, Leila /

ALEENA. First find out what your **Nanoo** did /

NOOR. Now, Leila /

ALEENA. Your **Nanoo** loves you, Leila, she does, but not like she loves them /

LEILA. Who? /

ALEENA. Shabana said she'd provide but she didn't, you scraped what you could from people round here /

LEILA. What? /

NOOR. Leave Shabana out of it /

ALEENA. Have you not heard?

Your precious Shabana, she's cleared off.

NOOR. **Bakwas.** Shabana wouldn't.

ALEENA. People are talking, they found out what her and Tariq did.

Beat.

Bogus packages for **Umrah** and **Hajj**?

Scamming people who are saving for a holy pilgrimage! She's gone.

NOOR. I don't believe you!

ALEENA. They should burn in hell /

NOOR. Liar! /

ALEENA. Shabana's gone, **Ami**!

LEILA. She's gone?

NOOR *rushes towards her phone, she dials Shabana's number, it no longer exists.*

ALEENA. She's a snake you never see coming.

NOOR. Leave this alone.

ALEENA. You both said you'd visit! That was part of the deal.

Beat.

LEILA. What?

Beat.

You did visit?

LEILA *looks at* NOOR.

Wednesdays?

Every Wednesday you got the train up there with Auntie Shabana?

Beat.

You did? Didn't you, **Nanoo**?

Beat.

What about all my letters? Auntie Shabana said Mum got them.

ALEENA *looks at* NOOR – *What letters?*

Beat.

ALEENA. Bastards.

NOOR. That's her aunt / and uncle

ALEENA. They're scum! They used me /

NOOR. Aleena /

ALEENA. My name –

NOOR. Aleena, **bas** /

ALEENA. No more **bas**, **Ami**!

Beat.

My name on the mortgage application.

NOOR. Don't.

Pause.

ALEENA. They needed another name on it, they wanted to buy a second house so those fuckers called me. That bastard Tariq stood over me, taught me how to knock up fake payslips. Once the bank found out they reported it the police.

Beat.

Judge charged me under section seven 'Supplying Articles for Use in Fraud'.

LEILA *looks at* NOOR *who doesn't look back.*

My signature, I get a third, I get paid, that was the deal, I did it for us after I lost my job /

NOOR. Tell her why you lost your job, tell her why you stopped going to work /

ALEENA. I couldn't get up in the mornings /

NOOR. Self-medicating, drinking on the job /

ALEENA. No! /

NOOR. You couldn't keep up with your rent, people found you passed out / in the middle of the street

ALEENA. Shut up, **Ami**! /

NOOR. Why? She's seen it all before, eight years old, picking you up from the kitchen floor, lit cigarettes burning through the carpet, God knows where she'd be if you hadn't / moved here

ALEENA. Yes thank you for saving us, **Ami**! Thank you thank you / thank you!

NOOR. No one forced you, Aleena, you knew what you were doing /

ALEENA. That money was for us so we could have a new life!

NOOR. You broke the law!

Beat

LEILA (*to* NOOR). You said it was drink driving?

NOOR *refuses to look at* LEILA.

ALEENA. When I got caught I was so scared. So I called your **Nanoo**. When I got here your Auntie Shabana was in the kitchen. She made me a cup of tea, rubbed my back, told me it was the best thing for everyone. We sat here for hours. The trial before the trial. My tea had gone cold by the time we had agreed /

LEILA. I don't want to / hear any more

NOOR. Leave this alone, Aleena!

ALEENA. Agreed to say that they had nothing to do with it, that it was all my idea.

Beat.

And what were your words, **Ami**?

Beat.

It's you, Aleena.

Beat.

It has to be you.

ALEENA *cries.*

Pause.

LEILA *looks at* NOOR.

LEILA. You sent her away?

Beat.

My mum?

Beat.

You chose them?

NOOR. The boys would have been without both parents if I hadn't.

LEILA. And me?

NOOR. I did what I thought was best.

LEILA. Best for them?

NOOR. For everyone.

LEILA. Do you love Rizwan and Hakim more than me?

NOOR. No, Leila.

LEILA. They made fun of my clothes last time and you didn't say anything! You never smile unless they phone! You talk to them, but you always tell me off.

NOOR. Because I'm trying to raise you, **Beta**.

LEILA. You lied!

Beat.

NOOR. I thought she might be safer in there, that she could be watched. This way I could look after you and Shabana could look after the boys, the rest I left in Allah's hands.

Beat.

When I went to visit her she didn't move, she just sat there, lifeless, a shell, it was the first and last time.

NOOR *cries.*

I told Shabana I couldn't go back there, not after what I…

Beat.

She gave me her word that she would send clothes and money and I wouldn't have to worry.

LEILA. You always told me to tell the truth, that it was **gunaah** to lie.

NOOR. I'm sorry.

LEILA. You're the liar.

NOOR *approaches* LEILA, LEILA *is reluctant to look at her.*

NOOR. We can get through this, **Jaan**. In time everything will be back to normal, **Beta**.

NOOR *grips* LEILA.

I'm not perfect I know, but I did this for us, for all of us.

LEILA. Us?

NOOR. My family, all of you, that's all I've ever wanted.

NOOR *holds* LEILA*'s face with both hands.*

If we don't forgive each other then who will.

LEILA *looks at* NOOR.

Forgive me, **Jaan**.

Beat.

ALEENA. Go and get your suitcase, Leila.

After a moment LEILA *exits into the hallway.* NOOR *and* ALEENA *are left alone in the space.*

Beat.

I'd tell you I felt sad, and you didn't do anything.

Beat.

You never asked me why.

Beat.

Why I cried for hours and hours.

Beat.

You left me alone with it

I've been alone since I can remember.

ALEENA *points to her head.*

Up here.

Beat.

You didn't tell us you loved us, not once, not even after Dad died.

NOOR. And when was I supposed to do that? I worked double shifts at that factory, twelve hours a day, my fingers bled, my feet were swollen all because he refused to get out of that chair, him and his 'depressive episodes'. You want to talk about loneliness, Aleena? Your father left me long before he died /

ALEENA. Dad never left you /

NOOR. He might as well have! My love was in my strength, my sacrifice. You knew you'd always have clothes on your back and food on the table. Does Leila?

ALEENA. She knows I love her.

NOOR. I sacrificed everything so you and Shabana could have a life here, with opportunities, prospects.

ALEENA. Debts and obligations.

NOOR. I made connections with whoever I could, I did what I had to do to.

ALEENA. You laid down like a dog.

I won't lay down for anyone and neither will Leila.

ALEENA *moves towards Shabana's picture.*

Why her?

Beat.

Because she stood by her husband?

Beat.

Because she had two boys?

Or is it because your grandsons weren't born out of wedlock?

NOOR. How simple do you think I am?

ALEENA *looks* NOOR *head on.*

Beat.

ALEENA. Then why did you choose me?

Beat.

NOOR. I've punished myself every day for it, if that's what you're trying to do then it's too late.

ALEENA *gestures to Shabana's picture.*

ALEENA. Is that what you crossed the sea for? For someone like *that* to speak for your **Izzat**?

Beat.

NOOR. You can't take her, Aleena, you know you can't.

ALEENA. Let me have this, **Ami**.

Beat.

NOOR. Have you ever asked her what *she* wants?

Really sat down and asked her.

Pause.

ALEENA. Tell me you love me, **Ami**.

Just once.

NOOR *is torn.*

You can't, can you?

Beat.

Every day I wake up and I don't know how I got here.

Whether the person I used to be even existed?

Dad was all I could think about, I lost the only person who ever understood me. I couldn't just move past it like you did.

NOOR. You think I moved past it? He was my husband.

ALEENA. You didn't cry once.

NOOR. You don't bare your soul in front of your children.

You give them space to bare theirs, *that's* motherhood.

ALEENA. That's cold.

ALEENA *cries.*

She would stand in front of me in her pyjamas and cry. I didn't know what to do, what sort of mother doesn't know what to do? You're supposed to just know, aren't you? She'd cry till she started to make that sound, you know that sound, **Ami**? When something's losing life? I couldn't sleep so I started the pills, they didn't touch the sides but the drink helped. No one was listening, no one was hearing me so I thought if I just held her, if I held her long enough she would stop, I thought if I gave her what I needed she wouldn't make that sound any more.

LEILA *silently stands by the doorway and watches, without her suitcase.*

I thought I'd know what to do with her, but it didn't come, it's never come, **Ami**.

ALEENA *sobs,* NOOR *watches her but can't quite reach her, after a moment* LEILA *speaks.*

LEILA. Mum?

ALEENA *wipes her tears.* ALEENA *looks at* LEILA *for a moment, she makes her way over to the sofa, she sits down and slips out a cigarette from her jacket pocket, she lights it.* ALEENA *pats the space next to her.*

ALEENA. Come here, Leila.

LEILA *joins* ALEENA *on the sofa.*

I don't think I've ever asked you.

LEILA. What?

ALEENA *glances over at* NOOR *then back to* LEILA.

ALEENA. I've never asked you what you want.

LEILA. You ask me that all the time.

ALEENA. Do I?

LEILA. You always ask me if I had a wish what would it be.

ALEENA. Wishes are a bit different, babe.

Beat.

What do you want, right now?

LEILA. I don't know.

ALEENA. You can tell me.

Beat.

LEILA. I want you to be happy.

ALEENA. Forget about me.

LEILA. This is stupid.

ALEENA. Try me.

Pause.

LEILA. I want it to go back to the way it was.

Beat.

ALEENA. Go on.

Beat.

LEILA. Back to when you and **Nanoo** used to laugh.

Beat.

Or when you'd come up behind her and wrap your arms around her while she made a cup of tea.

Beat.

When I'd watch you do your make-up while you had your morning coffee, or on Saturdays when you weren't at work and I'd put cucumbers on your eyes.

ALEENA *smiles.*

ALEENA. Leila's salon?

LEILA. And you'd give me one nice kiss instead of a thousand that sting.

Beat.

I want a proper long sleep with no bad dreams, and I don't want to jump when a door closes.

ALEENA *places her arm over* LEILA, LEILA *rests her head on* ALEENA*'s chest.*

ALEENA. Go on.

Beat.

LEILA. I want to go back to when I wasn't *your* reason for getting up in the morning, but *you* were mine.

Beat.

ALEENA. What else?

Beat.

LEILA. I don't want to be scared any more.

Beat.

NOOR. This is your home, **Jaan**, you belong here at your school, with your friends /

LEILA. You always think you know what's best, but you don't.

Beat.

You never stick up for me.

NOOR. Leila.

LEILA. You let everyone talk about me and talk for me.

Beat.

You think keeping me inside saying my **Namaz** and doing my coursework will make everything go away but it won't.

Beat.

And sometimes I hate you, I really hate you.

Beat.

You get it wrong, a lot.

Beat.

Things have to change, *you* have to change.

NOOR. Fine.

LEILA. You've got a lot to learn.

NOOR. Okay, Leila.

I know.

LEILA *turns to* ALEENA.

LEILA. What do you want, Mum?

Beat.

ALEENA. I want to give you everything you just asked for.

Beat.

LEILA. And you will.

Pause.

(*Hopeful.*) I'll come and see you all the time, half term, weekends, we can get our nails done, eat quarter pounders with cheese.

ALEENA. Onions and ketchup?

LEILA. You'll be okay, Mum, you're the bravest person I've met.

ALEENA. You think?

LEILA. I know.

Beat.

ALEENA *gives* LEILA *a kiss on her forehead then tears herself away.*

ALEENA. Sian said we hurt the ones we love most /

Silly that.

She said 'don't overestimate freedom, Ally,' scary init, **Ami**? /

NOOR. Yes.

But it's our right.

Beat.

I'm sorry I took it away.

ALEENA *is surprised by* NOOR*'s response, she gives* NOOR *a forgiving nod.* ALEENA *picks up her duffle bag, she looks at* LEILA *and holds her arms out,* LEILA *hugs* ALEENA.

LEILA. Wait for me, Mum.

ALEENA *looks at every part of* LEILA*'s face.*

ALEENA. Always, bubba.

ALEENA *does the butterfly across her cheek one last time.* LEILA *smiles.* ALEENA *tears herself away,* LEILA *stands next to* NOOR. ALEENA *moves towards the door.* NOOR *goes to reach for her but stops.*

NOOR. Aleena?

ALEENA *stops without turning around.*

ALEENA. I'm doing my best, **Ami**.

My best.

Beat.

NOOR. I know.

Beat.

ALEENA *bravely faces* NOOR.

ALEENA. I love you, **Ami**.

Beat.

NOOR. I love you too.

Pause.

Jaan.

LEILA *beams a smile.*

Blackout.

Glossary

Nano – Grandmother
Masjid – mosque
Kapray Phenno – put your clothes on
Jaan – my life
Ami – Mother
Hawa – wind
Sooraj – sun
Beta/beti – child
Apna Moun Kholo – open your mouth
Kholo Nah – open it
Jhoot – liar
Bas – enough / that's enough
Bakwas – foolish talk
To Kya – so what?
Allah yah reh tah he – God lives here
Sharabi – alcoholic
Mashallah – what God has willed, in the sense of 'what God has willed has happened'; it is used to say something good has happened
Behn – sister
Koi Bhat Nay – don't worry
Fajr – Morning Prayer
Inshallah – God willing
Bilkul – certainly
Hum sara ekh he – we are all one
Hudafis – goodbye
Sabar – paticncc
Shukriya – thank you
Shabash – well done
Gunaah – sin
Maaf kar dain – forgive him / her
Woh ek Besharam Larhki he! – she's a shameless girl!
Tum Pagal hogh ho?! – have you gone mad?
Leh! – see!
Chup – quiet
Badtameez – someone who has bad manners
Izzat – honour

A Nick Hern Book

Favour first published as a paperback original in Great Britain in 2022 by Nick Hern Books Limited, The Glasshouse, 49a Goldhawk Road, London W12 8QP, in association with the Bush Theatre, London, and Clean Break

Cover image: Studio Doug

Designed and typeset by Nick Hern Books, London
Printed in Great Britain by Mimeo Ltd, Huntingdon, Cambridgeshire PE29 6XX

A CIP catalogue record for this book is available from the British Library

ISBN 978 1 83904 091 7